1 0 0
Favorite
Plants
For Shade

100
Favorite
Plants
For Shade

TERI DUNN

MetroBooks

DEDICATION

For my mother-in-law, Carol Dunn, whose shade garden is a peaceful haven where kitties, herons, and grandchildren love to roam.

Thanks to the Petherbridge family, Kathy Pyle (again), Marraine Gaul, Randy the Fedex guy, Gordon Morrison, and Shawn, Wes, and Tris.

MetroBooks

An Imprint of Friedman/Fairfax Publishers

©1999 by Michael Friedman Publishing Group, Inc.

Library of Congress Cataloging-in-Publication Data available upon request.

ISBN 1-56799-653-1

Editor: Susan Lauzau
Art Director: Jeff Batzli
Layout Designer: Meredith Miller
Photography Editor: Jennifer L. Bove
Production Manager: Niall Brennan

Color separations by Ocean Graphic International Company Ltd.
Printed in Singapore by KHL Printing Co Pte Ltd.

1 3 5 7 9 10 8 6 4 2

For bulk purchases and special sales, please contact:
Friedman/Fairfax Publishers
Attention: Sales Department
15 West 26th Street
New York, NY 10010
212/685-6610 FAX 212/685-1307

Visit our website:
http://www.metrobooks.com

Photography credits:

A-Z Botannical: ©Malcolm Richards: p. 90

©R. Todd Davis: pp. 94, 113

©Derek Fell: pp. 42, 92

Garden Picture Library: ©Brian Carter: p. 96; ©Christopher Fairweather: p. 83; ©John Glover: p.117; ©Howard Rice: p. 72; ©Gary Rogers: p. 78

©Dency Kane: pp. 16, 19, 21, 23, 30, 35, 36, 37, 50, 56, 66, 70, 80, 87, 89, 95, 99, 102, 109, 110, 114

©Charles Mann: pp. 6, 13, 17, 29, 31, 32, 39, 45, 59, 60, 61, 62, 69, 71, 74, 75, 77, 82, 101, 115

©Clive Nichols: pp. 9, 76

©Jerry Pavia: pp. 2, 10, 11, 14, 20, 22, 24, 25, 26, 27, 34, 38, 41, 43, 44, 46, 47, 48, 49, 51, 52, 53, 54, 55, 57, 58, 63, 64, 65, 67, 68, 73, 79, 84, 85, 86, 91, 93, 97, 98, 103, 105, 107, 108, 111, 112, 116

©Joanne Pavia: pp. 12, 15, 18, 28, 40, 81, 88

Visuals Unlimited: ©Bill Beatty: p. 33; ©Derrick Ditchburn: p. 100; ©John Gerlach: p. 106; ©Jeffrey Howe: p. 104

CONTENTS

Introduction

Judging from many gardening books and magazines, a beautiful garden is full of sunshine and colorful flowers. Does this mean that shade on your property means no garden? Not at all! Here are one hundred plants that will prosper in shade, from a woodland's deepest gloom, to the space under a small grove of trees, to areas that get morning sun and afternoon shade. Many plants appropriate for shade have extraordinarily beautiful leaves—there's amazing variety in shape, texture, and even color. And you may be pleasantly surprised to discover, as you thumb through the following pages, that many also have attractive flowers.

Shade actually is a benefit to many plants. Lack of direct sun means their leaves look healthy and lush, without burned edges or tips, without drying out and wilting. Sunlight also tends to bleach out the beauty of variegated leaves, leaves that are marked or rimmed in white, cream, or gold, whereas in shade such foliage thrives and lights up the scene. Shelter from the sun's hot rays also preserves flower color, so shade bloomers often hold their color very well. And if you have the impression that plants that flower in shade come only in white, feast your eyes on the upcoming pages: you'll see every hue of yellow, blue, pink, purple, and red. Such variety, both in foliage and flower, suggests all sorts of exciting possibilities. Rather than wondering what on earth to grow in shade, you are invited to view a range of tantalizing choices.

TYPES OF SHADE

Before you start landscaping your shade garden, take a moment to analyze it. Each entry in this book addresses what sort of shade is best for the plant in question. Of course, there is always latitude, and something described as ideal for "dappled shade" may well please you growing in half-day shade, or more.

That said, here are the three main types of shade gardeners contend with.

Full shade: This is defined as an area where foliage from overhead trees or an adjacent structure (house, outbuilding, deck) effectively blocks out practically all light, all

day. If the shade comes from trees, the deprivation to plants below is more severe because their dense or overlapping leaves may also keep rainwater from reaching the ground, and their roots may suck out moisture and nutrients from the soil at their feet (common culprits are Norway and silver maples, oaks, and many evergreens). Full shade is not easy to garden in, no doubt about it. But with some soil improvement (described in the following pages), regular watering, and carefully chosen plants, you have every chance of beautifying such a spot.

Dappled, filtered, or partial shade: You find this pleasant condition under deciduous trees with lighter-textured foliage (such as birches, locusts, olives, and shorter growers like dogwoods and hawthorns). A pergola or overhead lathwork also will cause this effect. The constant shifting of light and shadows goes on for most of the day, giving shade plants below the best of both worlds—sufficient light to photosynthesize and bloom, but protection from the sun's damaging rays.

Half shade: As alluded to above, many shady gardens actually get several hours of full sun. At other times of the day, the sun moves around the house, garage, wall, fence, or bordering wooded area, and shadows fall over the area. Shade plants seem to do best when the sunny period is in the morning, rather than the reverse, because afternoon sun tends to be hotter and more intense. Lots of plants like half shade, even ones usually billed as sun lovers. But every yard is different, so experiment and find out what works and what you like.

CHANGING SHADE

No matter what type of shade you have, expect it to change. The situation often just gets darker and darker as your trees grow taller and broader (or vines envelop your pergola). Sometimes an unexpected storm takes out limbs or an entire tree and suddenly there's light where there never was any before. If your shade plants become established where you've planted them, they likely will adapt. If light becomes too dim, they may flower less or cease flowering, grow lanky as they stretch toward a bit of sun, or roam into areas that suit them better. Take all this in stride. In the words of the late great garden writer Henry Mitchell, "If you stop and think of it ... [plants] would be much better off if we stopped pestering them all the time."

There may be times when you tamper with the shade you've been given. Sometimes you simply have to. Lower limbs on your evergreens lose all their needles and eventually die; you might as well remove them. Damaged or diseased branches on evergreens and deciduous trees alike should be removed promptly. First-aid pruning can generally be done at any time, though evergreens tend to bleed if cut in late spring or early summer when their sap is running. Better to wait until late summer or early autumn when the evergreen is heading into dormancy.

TOO MUCH SHADE

If you want to admit more sunlight into a wooded area and don't want to take out entire trees, judicious pruning will help. Don't get in there and hack away indiscriminately. Most trees recover well from pruning as long as no more than a quarter or at most a third of their growth is removed in any one growing season. So, if you have major thinning in mind, spread the work over several seasons.

It is admittedly painful to cut down a tree to make way for a garden. But you ought to consider it if the area you have in mind hosts a black walnut or ailanthus; both of these secrete chemicals that harm or kill neighboring plants. If you decide to leave them, the situation is not hopeless, but you will have to do research and endure plenty of trial and error until you succeed in calling the area in their vicinity a shade garden.

Less obvious roadblocks to success are shallow-rooted trees, among them maples, cottonwoods, and spruce. These are resource hogs, sapping moisture and nutrients from the top layers of soil. And your shade plants need only the first six to twelve inches (15 to 30cm) of soil to grow in. Your options? Remove some (but not all?) such trees. Make raised beds or place plants in containers around the area. Or garden well away from the root zones of the trees.

TOO LITTLE SHADE

Suppose you want to make shade. You've just built a new house or moved into a new housing development, and the lot is distressingly bare. You need some relief from the blasting rays of the sun.

Quick coverage, of course, can be provided by building something. A pergola, with slats that admit some sun, is attractive. If you can, site it on the south side of the house, where the light is strongest.

Alternatively, plant some shade trees. While none can truly be termed "fast growing," some are quicker than others, so you can hope to enjoy shade—and a shade garden—sometime in the next decade. Good choices are dogwoods, Japan-ese maples, Russian olive, sourwood, and chaste tree. For more ideas, and for information on proper planting techniques (soil amendments will be key), consult your local nursery.

DON'T TOUCH!

One thing you should never do with your shade area is to remove autumn leaves. In nature, they aren't raked up, are they? Instead, they break down and contribute valuable humus to the soil. If you observe that they have fallen in overwhelming numbers or their broad leaves are forming a slimy, smothering mat, intervene by gently raking out some piles and composting them or dicing them up with the lawn-mower or in a shredder—then, return this precious resource to the place it came from. Your shade plants will be ever so grateful.

GROWING SHADE PLANTS

The secret to successful shade gardening is the same as with any other type of gardening: good soil equals happy plants. You cannot just plunk in a groundcover or shade-loving wildflower, walk away, and expect it to thrive. The unfortunate fact is that the soil under trees or on the north side of the garage may not be very good, and when you have plans for the area, you should invest some effort in initial improvement and be prepared to keep at it in ensuing seasons.

Many shade plants adore humusy soil, which helps retain soil moisture and improves soil texture. So dig in organic matter in the form of compost, damp peat moss, decomposed leaves, or dehydrated manure. The result will be hospitable ground that gets seedlings off to a good start and nurtures them in years to come. Note that young plants often don't bloom or appear to grow much at all in their first season; this is because they are busy forming roots that will fuel future growth.

You'll notice that the descriptions of some of the plants in this book point out special requirements—damp or moist soil is recommended, or acidic soil is preferred. You may have such conditions naturally on your property, but a little soil preparation prior to planting is still wise.

Soil moisture can become a real issue. It seems spring is often damp, and, when summer ushers in, the soil dries out. Some shade plants respond by going dormant, literally disappearing until the following year; others may simply die out. To a certain extent, the soil improvement recommended above will improve moisture retention. Mulching also can help. But you may have to visit your shade garden with the hose or a sprinkler—so, hopefully, water is within reach. Some gardeners choose to lay down soaker hoses, which by virtue of the dimmer light don't seem as obtrusive in the shade as they do in sunny spots.

One last note about the care of your shade plants: Feeding, generally speaking, is not mandatory. If the light is right, the soil is good, and the moisture levels are adequate, you can be sure your shade plants will thrive and contribute interest and glory to your garden.

Aegopodium podagraria

Bishop's goutweed

HEIGHT/WIDTH: 1'–2' (30–60cm)/spreading habit

FLOWERS: white umbels

BLOOM TIME: early summer

ZONES: 4–9

'Variegatum' bishop's goutweed

This is a common plant that sophisticated horticulturists love to hate. "Weedy," they say, "ugly," they sneer. Well, beauty is in the eye of the beholder—and there are times and places when bishop's goutweed is just the plant you need. It is one of the few plants that will grow in terrible soil in complete or partial shade, with no attention from you. It's suitable for a neglected or problem area on your property that needs quick and thorough coverage.

Bishop's goutweed is most often seen in its variegated form, 'Variegatum', and the leaves are actually rather pretty. They're usually lime green and edged liberally with creamy white, making them "pop" in gloomy spots. The flower heads are plentiful and attractive enough, though too small to be dramatic. To control the plant, yank out or whack back unwanted growth and, if you're willing to take the time, cut out the flowers before they go to seed. If you like the plant's look and want to enjoy it in controlled circumstances, containers are the way to go.

The plant is originally from Europe and must owe its name to the fact that it grows around medieval monasteries and churches. It was probably deliberately planted long ago as a medicinal plant, and used to treat gout as well as sore joints and other aches.

Ageratum houstonianum

Ageratum

HEIGHT/WIDTH: 6"–14" × 6"–14" (15–35.5cm × 15–35.5cm)

FLOWERS: blue, pink, or white

BLOOM TIME: summer

ZONES: all zones (annual)

'Blue Horizon' ageratum

For fast color in dappled shade, few plants beat this bullet-proof annual. It forms small, compact mounds of mint green leaves and, for the entire summer and well into autumn, displays loads of neat color. All it requires is decent, well-drained soil; it survives in drier soils, too, but is not as attractive.

Ageratum's flower heads are clusters of up to forty little fluffy blooms. Most of us have seen the plant in blue or lilac-blue, and sometimes this hue is exactly what you need—as an edging for a hosta border, perhaps, or skirting some spring-flowering shrubs after their blooms have gone by. But it also comes in perky white ('Album', 'Hawaii White') and even pink (the dwarf 'Swing Pink'), suggesting other planting possibilities. A combination of these, rib-boned through a shady perennial bed or along a path, would be lovely.

If you need further persuasion: ageratum attracts but-terflies, creatures not often seen in shady spots.

Ajuga reptans

Ajuga, bugleweed

HEIGHT/WIDTH: 4"–8" × 8" (10–20cm × 20cm)

FLOWERS: purple or blue spikes

BLOOM TIME: late spring–early summer

ZONES: 3–8

'Burgundy Glow' ajuga

As a groundcover, this plant has become a bit of a cliché and can spread quite aggressively. But it really has many good and useful qualities, and it should not be written off altogether. Ajuga often grows very well where few other plants thrive, even sites with thin or poor soil, or areas of deep shade. It spreads out well, by means of creeping runners. Its only shortcoming is susceptibility to fungus and rot, but these can be avoided by planting it in well-drained soil.

Nowadays, ajuga comes in a variety of intriguing forms, so if you search the nurseries or catalogs diligently, you can make yourself the proud owner of a truly handsome, unique, low-maintenance planting. Among the many choices are 'Burgundy Glow', whose leaves are splashed with pink and cream; 'Pink Surprise', with lance-shaped leaves of bronze-green (and pinkish flowers); and 'Purple Brocade', sporting especially ruffled duotone leaves of purple-bronze and forest green. The most interesting one is 'Catlin's Giant', which has extra-big, dark bronze–purple leaves and taller flowers (it originated in the garden of a fellow who accidentally sprayed weed killer on his ajuga patch—most of the plants died, but one clump survived and came back in this jumbo size).

Alchemilla mollis

Lady's-mantle

HEIGHT/WIDTH: 1'–2' × 1'–2' (30–60cm × 30–60cm)

FLOWERS: tiny sprays; chartreuse

BLOOM TIME: late spring–early summer

ZONES: 4–8

Lady's-mantle

As a foliage plant, lady's-mantle is especially desirable. The large, scallop-edged leaves (up to 4 inches [10cm] across) are lime green and have a soft, felted texture. When it rains or when early morning dew gathers on the leaves, the water beads up like quicksilver—a truly enchanting sight. The leaves are borne in clumps and lend an immediate grace and softness to semishady areas.

The frothy flowers also make a welcome contribution. They are a sharp, clear shade of yellow-green, best described as chartreuse. They appear in profusion each spring, and continue to a lesser extent for the rest of the season. Short stalks hold them slightly above and away from the leaves. Their form and color mix nicely with other shade bloomers, particularly violet or rosy flowers, such as those of creeping phlox and some violas.

Lady's-mantle is simple to grow. All it needs is moist but well-drained soil. If your summers become hot and dry, provide a mulch and supplemental water.

Amsonia tabernaemontana

Bluestar

HEIGHT/WIDTH: 2'–3' × 2'–3' (60–90cm × 60–90cm)

FLOWERS: clusters of blue stars

BLOOM TIME: early summer

ZONES: 3–9

Bluestar

At maturity, bluestar gains an appealingly soft, shrubby appearance that is welcome in semishady spots. And its blooms are that hard-to-find shade of true blue. They are about half an inch (1.5cm) across and star-shaped, and appear in domed clusters at the tops of the stems. The tidy foliage, between 3 and 6 inches (7.5 and 15cm) long, is narrow and willowy and encircles the erect stems.

Despite its seemingly delicate appearance, bluestar thrives in moderately fertile soil and proves itself to be drought tolerant over long summers. If it gets leggy, trim it back occasionally to keep growth dense. Bluestar is also usually free of disease and pest problems. Autumn foliage is a real plus: instead of fading away, the leaves turn a vibrant shade of gold that brings a welcome glow.

This handsome plant is probably best grown in groups or sweeps, so its fine texture won't be lost and the wonderful shade of blue has a chance to really stand out. It's a striking companion for orange- or red-flowered deciduous azaleas, which generally bloom at the same time.

Anemone nemorosa

Wood anemone

HEIGHT/WIDTH: 3"–6" × 6"–12" (7.5–15cm × 15–30cm)

FLOWERS: blue or white

BLOOM TIME: spring

ZONES: 4–8

Wood anemone

While other members of the vast anemone tribe may tolerate light or part-day shade, the wood anemone, a wildflower of European origins, is particularly prized. It is not a tall plant, though it presents its lovely, starry blooms to advantage above its palmate foliage. Moderately moist, rich soil, as is often found in woodland gardens, inspires it to grow lustily. As such, it is ideal for naturalizing.

There are quite a few cultivars to choose from—your best bet is to comb specialty catalogs—but most are in the white or blue range. 'Robinsoniana' (named for the renowned English plantsman William Robinson) is widely regarded as a classic and features large, ½-inch (4cm) blooms in pale lilac, with silvery undersides and a puffball of soft yellow stamens in the middle. Also lovely is the shining white 'Alba' (an heirloom variety that has been around since 1771!) and its double form, 'Alba Plena'.

Although it doesn't grow from a bulb, but rather from a stoloniferous rootstock, this anemone is best planted in autumn, about 3 inches (7.5cm) deep in humusy soil. This gives it a head start, and it may just bloom for you its first spring. It generally dies down (goes dormant) during the summer months.

Aquilegia × hybrida

Columbine

HEIGHT/WIDTH: 2'–3' × 1'–2' (60–90cm × 30–60cm)

FLOWERS: various colors

BLOOM TIME: spring–early summer

ZONES: 3–9

McKana Giants columbine

Columbine flowers are so lovely that no shade gardener should do without them. The plants do best in decent, well-drained soil, and like a little morning sun or dappled sunlight. They make charming companions for hostas and ferns. Just bear in mind that, even in the best settings, they are short-lived. But the species will self-sow; and, if you grow one of the hybrids, you won't hesitate to run right out and replace it.

The original red-and-yellow wild columbine (*A. canadensis*) has small, nodding, upside-down blossoms. Generally, the spurred outer petals are red and the fluted inner ones bright yellow.

There are a host of fabulous, tall, multicolored hybrids to choose from. Many are bicolors, which makes for a lively display. Perhaps the best of the hybrids are the McKana

Giants, which grow to between 2 and 3 feet (60 and 90cm) tall and carry lots of extra-big flowers, in many color combinations. The durable 'Biedermeier' strain is about half as tall, but has an equally diverse color range. If you prefer solid-color columbines, there are plenty to choose from, from sherbet yellow 'Maxistar' to pristine white 'Snow Queen'.

Columbine's only flaw is that its lacy foliage is prone to leaf miners, which weave their trails inside the leaves until little green is left. The flowers keep on blooming, though, seemingly unaffected. Remove all affected foliage, or wait until flowering is over and cut the entire plant down. A fresh flush of new foliage will appear shortly after.

Arisaema triphyllum

Jack-in-the-pulpit

HEIGHT/WIDTH: 2'–3' × 1' (60–90cm × 30cm)

FLOWERS: spadix, color varies

BLOOM TIME: spring

ZONES: 4–8

Jack-in-the-pulpit

This North American woodland native has an eccentrically elegant look that has captured the imaginations of adventurous shade gardeners. Good news: it is also relatively easy to grow. A sheltered spot in moist soil is essential. It is slow and tedious from seed, taking up to four years to reach blooming size. Better to start with a seedling that has already developed its small bulblike root, called a corm. These are available from nurseries in the spring.

Each Jack-in-the-pulpit plant grows two stalks; one bears a pair of leaf-topped stems, the other bears the odd-looking flowering structure. A green and maroon striped hood that curves over at the top, the "pulpit," shields "Jack," a slender, dark red-brown, greenish yellow, or white spadix.

The true flowers lurk at the bottom of the spadix and are very tiny. Through it all, the broad leaves, borne in leaflets of three, form a canopy over and nearly hide this show.

In autumn, if the plant is growing in rich, moist soil and prospering, a cluster of oval red berries appears, sheathed in a papery cylinder. The berries are not edible.

If this plant captures your fancy, you will be intrigued to learn that it has many Asian relatives that are only now making it into the offerings of specialty catalogs. Some have textured or marbled foliage and stems (marketed as "snake-like"!). There are dramatic variations in the "Jack" and "pulpit" colors, and a few have orange autumn berries.

Aruncus dioicus

Goatsbeard

HEIGHT/WIDTH: 4'–7' × 3'–4' (120–210cm × 90–120cm)

FLOWERS: white panicles

BLOOM TIME: late spring–early summer

ZONES: 2–6

Goatsbeard

No, it's not a big astilbe, though you would be pardoned for thinking so the first time you see goatsbeard. It even likes the same conditions of full to partial shade and moist soil. But goatsbeard is a much larger plant, attaining a size and stature that is downright shrublike. Staking is not usually necessary.

Goatsbeard's flowers are not as long-blooming as those of astilbe, but the show is so magnificent you may not mind. For a couple of weeks in late spring or early summer, the stately, feathery wands of creamy white flowers rise in a flurry above the light green foliage. The male and female flowers are borne on separate plants; the male flowers are fuller and the female ones are more greenish. Unfortunately, nurseries don't differentiate, and you won't know until it blooms. Better to plant several, then.

After the dramatic flowers pass, you'll still appreciate the plant for its foliage. The delicate, textured leaves are compound, dissected, and toothed, and they clothe the plant from head to toe. They are untroubled by pests and look fresh all season. If the species is too big for your purposes, seek out the shorter cultivars 'Child of Two Worlds' (3 to 4 feet [90–120cm]) or 'Kneiffi' (3 feet [90cm]).

Asarum canadense

Wild ginger

HEIGHT/WIDTH: 4"–12" × 4"–6" (10–30cm × 10–15cm)

FLOWERS: tiny; purplish brown

BLOOM TIME: spring

ZONES: 4–8

Wild ginger

This is the native North American version of the similar European ginger. Like its relative, it has handsome, dark green, heart-shaped leaves and likes to grow in moist, rich soil. But its leaves are usually larger, up to 6 inches (15cm) across, and have a slightly furry (thus, less glossy) texture. The broader leaves give the plant, as a groundcover, a bolder presence. For instance, it is better able to hold its own in the company of hostas, or to make a dramatic pathside swath. American ginger, unfortunately, seems to be a bit more susceptible to slug damage, so be on the lookout.

Another significant difference is that the leaves of the American ginger are not evergreen over the winter. Even so, they return with gusto each spring. And, generally speaking, the plant is tougher than its European counterpart. Although it is deciduous, it is hardier—gardeners in the North will have better luck with it. It also has proven to take the heat and humidity of a southern summer better.

The small flowers, nondescript, purplish brown, bell-shaped curiosities, are borne in the spring and are well hidden by the foliage. The plant may self-sow, but it spreads mainly by creeping roots. Speaking of the roots, they have a distinctly gingerlike scent and flavor, and were used by native tribes in cooking and medicinally. But the plant is not related to commercial ginger root.

Asarum europaeum

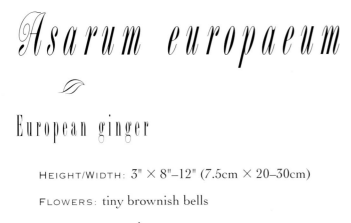

European ginger

HEIGHT/WIDTH: 3" × 8"–12" (7.5cm × 20–30cm)

FLOWERS: tiny brownish bells

BLOOM TIME: spring

ZONES: 4–8

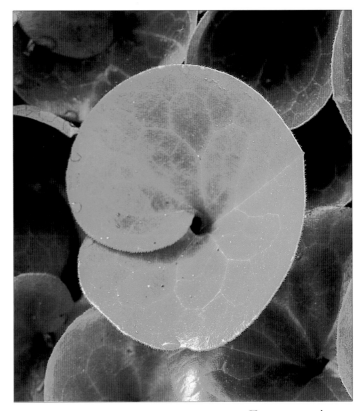

European ginger

If you're looking to densely carpet a shady area with an evergreen groundcover that looks great all season, resists pests and diseases, and requires little or no attention, European ginger is an elegant choice. The kidney-shaped leaves are rich green and wonderfully glossy. Plus, the plant grows and multiplies quickly.

The only catch is that the soil must be right in order to get a good performance. It should be on the moist side, humusy, and yet well drained, so the plants don't suffer from "wet feet." Furthermore, European ginger tends to prefer slightly acidic conditions. Woodland gardens in the Northeast probably fit this bill the best; gardeners else-where can try their luck by meeting as many of these conditions as possible.

Ginger's flowers are not a reason to grow the plant, for they are hidden under the leaves; but they are fascinating. They are tiny things, reddish inside, gray-green outside; one botanist aptly likened them to "little brown stone crocks." They last many weeks, and, when they pass, the seeds are carried off by small rodents.

The plant gets its name from its root, which has an appealing, gingerlike scent and flavor. It is not related to commercial ginger root.

Astilbe × *arendsii*

Astilbe

HEIGHT/WIDTH: 1½'–4' × 1½'–2½' (45–120cm × 45–75cm)

FLOWERS: plumes (many colors)

BLOOM TIME: spring–summer

ZONES: 4–9

'Gloria Purpurea' astilbe

Where they can be grown—in fertile, moist, well-drained soil, in parts of the country not given to extremes of heat or humidity—there are no finer shade-loving plants than astilbes. A great many of the best varieties were bred in Germany at the turn of the century by accomplished plants-man George Arends. The magnificent feathery plumes, actually masses of tiny flowers, come in a range of colors, from white to lavender to pink to red. Bloom times vary, so if you plan carefully, you can enjoy a long period of color.

Planted in a sweep in a woodland setting or even as a formal circle around the base of a tree, astilbes are delightful. They are also a popular choice for along the banks of a pool, pond, or stream.

After the flowers go by, the plant remains attractive. A clump-former, astilbe is clothed in toothed leaflets that look somewhat ferny. Problems with diseases and pests are rare.

Athyrium goeringianum 'Pictum'

(A. niponicum 'Pictum')

Japanese painted fern

HEIGHT/WIDTH: 1'–2' × 6"–10" (30–60cm × 15–25.5cm)

FLOWERS: none

BLOOM TIME: not applicable

ZONES: 5–8

Japanese painted fern

Unlike the vast majority of ferns, Japanese painted fern has handsomely variegated foliage. The fronds are pewtery-silver with a green border; the veins are plum or wine red. Although Japanese painted fern still needs shade to truly thrive, the more light the fronds receive, the more intense the coloring appears. You can experiment with this quality by moving a plant around from one year to the next (or in a container, certainly), or by observing the changes it makes from early spring to late summer, assuming the type of shade it receives varies. The show is enhanced by reddish stems.

This is not an especially hardy fern, and it will not only brown but also die back in a cold autumn and winter. If you are growing it in a marginal climate, either dig it up and bring it in for the winter, or try a heavy protective mulch. Either way, it won't remain evergreen over the winter, though you can look forward to a fresh flush of growth the next spring, heralded by the appearance of new, tiny, rosy-red fiddleheads.

This attractive fern is a favorite with gardeners who grow spring-blooming bulbs and wildflowers. You can see why: the fronds expand just in time to hide and distract from the dying-back foliage. Japanese painted fern also adds fascination to hosta beds, and makes a neat and lovely edging for a somewhat formal shady border.

Begonia grandis

Hardy begonia

HEIGHT/WIDTH: 1'–2' × 1'–2' (30–60cm × 30–60cm)

FLOWERS: sprays, pink or white

BLOOM TIME: summer

ZONES: 6–10

Hardy begonia

It looks like a houseplant begonia, perhaps one of the angel-wing types, but this is truly a hardy plant, suitable for growing outdoors and leaving out over the winter in many places. The leaves are big and jagged in form; their top sides are dappled with rich purple, with a velvety red reverse. The dainty little flowers, usually pink, sometimes pink-tinged white, appear later in the season in clusters, when color is often in short supply. (There is a white-flowered variant, 'Alba'.)

To keep hardy begonia looking good, grow it in moist but well-drained soil. Yes, this versatile plant will do well even in full shade. If happy, hardy begonia will spread eagerly by means of little bulbils that are shed by the stems later in the season. You can intercept these if you have other plans for them (you may wish to plant them in another spot or give some to a friend) or want to control the plant's expansion.

If you are at all concerned about your plants making it through the cold weather, give them a mulch in late autumn. As long as the tuberous roots don't freeze, they'll return in full glory the next year.

Begonia × tuberhybrida

Tuberous begonia

HEIGHT/WIDTH: 1'–2' × 1'–2' (30–60cm × 30–60cm)

FLOWERS: color varies

BLOOM TIME: summer

ZONES: 9–10 (grown as an annual)

Tuberous begonia

These are the jumbo-flowered sensations you see so vigorously advertised every spring in nursery catalogs and garden centers. They are touted as a dependable source of bold color for partial to full shade, which is true. The plump, 4- to 5-inch (10 to 13cm) blooms come in a range of bright colors (red, orange, yellow, hot pink) as well as white and picotee (white or cream petals, with colorful edging) and lace (colorful petals, white or cream edging). A happy plant will bloom like gangbusters.

Many gardeners like to grow these in containers, window boxes, hanging baskets, and so forth. As long as the plants get what they need, namely a good, rich soil mix, adequate moisture, and decent air circulation, they do well. You can also plant the tubers in the ground, realizing that they are tender and will die over the winter unless you overwinter them in a cool (not freezing) place in baggies of sawdust or moss.

If you get hooked on using these in your shade garden, it might behoove you to do some shopping around. Not all tuberous begonias are created equal. Some are propagated vegetatively to assure uniformity, others are seed-grown, with the expected variations. Some have smaller flowers, some bloom longer. The best are the Blackmore & Langdon strain, from England but available abroad from select nurseries. Also worthwhile are the widely available U.S.-bred tuberous begonias out of the Santa Cruz, California, area.

Bergenia cordifolia

Bergenia

HEIGHT/WIDTH: 1'–1½' × 1' (30–45cm × 30cm)

FLOWERS: pink, red, white

BLOOM TIME: spring

ZONES: 3–8

'Redstart' bergenia

Looking almost tropical in its lushness, bergenia forms big, bold, cabbagelike clumps with sturdy, glossy leaves. Each leaf is oval or heart-shaped, and can be as wide as a foot (30cm) across. The texture is leathery and shiny, and the foliage develops brown edges only if the plants get too much sun in the summer or if you neglect to mulch them for a harsh winter. Otherwise, bergenia is handsome in all seasons, remaining evergreen in most parts of the country. The onset of cool autumn weather inspires the leaves to turn an attractive shade of bronze, russet, or purple. This plant is a dramatic choice for mass plantings, such as under a tree, at the base of a shrub border, or along a walkway.

The flowers appear just above the leaves in spring, on strong stalks, and consist of lush trusses of bright pink blossoms. There are a number of worthy hybrids. The handsome Bressingham selections, 'Bressingham Ruby', 'Bressingham Salmon', 'Bressingham White', hail from England and can be found in some U.S. nurseries. Widely available hybrids include 'Abendglut' ('Evening Glow'), with flowers that are nearly crimson and foliage that turns maroon in winter; 'Perfecta', with rosy-red flowers and purplish leaves; and 'Silberlicht' ('Silver Light'), with pink-blushed white flowers with red centers.

Browallia speciosa

Browallia

HEIGHT/WIDTH: 1'–2' × 8"–10" (30–60cm × 20–30cm)

FLOWERS: usually blue

BLOOM TIME: summer

ZONES: 9–10 (annual in all other zones)

Browallia

Since browallia, also called bush violet, is of tropical origins, it's best grown in the Deep South, Gulf Coast, or mild areas of the West. The rest of us can envy those gardeners, or enjoy it as an annual. Because of its arching, drooping stems, it's also suitable for containers or hanging baskets, perhaps on a protected porch. In any event, don't allow it to be exposed to hot afternoon sun, which causes leaf-tip burn. Filtered shade is best, and the soil should be evenly moist.

The somewhat sticky leaves are long (up to 4 inches [10cm]), with pointed tips, and browallia is more upright than spreading—though this characteristic is not obvious when it is grown in a grouping or as a groundcover.

Browallia is blanketed in bell-shaped, 1- or 2-inch (2.5 or 5cm) blooms for much of the summer, and they are beauties. Usually lilac blue, they are also available in deep violet-blue ('Marine Bells', 'Blue Bells') and white, which really lights up semishady areas ('White Troll', 'White Bells'). Newly introduced 'Vanja' has vivid blue flowers with white eyes.

Brunnera macrophylla

Brunnera, Siberian bugloss, perennial forget-me-not

HEIGHT/WIDTH: 1'–2' × 1'–2' (30–60cm × 30–60cm)

FLOWERS: sprays of tiny blue flowers

BLOOM TIME: late spring–early summer

ZONES: 3–7

Brunnera

If you love forget-me-nots, try this vigorous-growing perennial charmer. Loose sprays of tiny (¼-inch [6mm]), star-shaped, brilliant blue flowers appear early, along with the spring bulbs and forsythia, and bloom with abandon for up to a month. The plant makes a wonderful "weaver" in areas where you've planted a variety of flowers, because the color goes with almost everything. It also brings fresh excitement to hosta or fern beds in semishade. White-flowered brunneras are available, as are ones with variegated leaves (ivory-banded 'Hadspen Cream' is a stunner). Note that the plant will self-sow, though it's simple to pull out unwanted volunteers.

Even if it didn't flower, brunnera would be a valuable addition to a lightly shaded garden as a groundcover, because its heart-shaped leaves are attractive in their own right. They start out small, form a pretty carpet that disguises fading bulb foliage, and expand in size (sometimes to nearly 8 inches [20cm] across) as the summer goes by. Watch out for nibbling slugs, though, and set out bait if they start to disfigure the planting.

Caladium bicolor

(C. hortulanum)

Caladium, elephant's ears

HEIGHT/WIDTH: 1'–2' × 1'–2' (30–60cm × 30–60cm)

FLOWERS: greenish-white spathes

BLOOM TIME: spring

ZONES: 9–10 (annual elsewhere)

'Fannie Munson' caladium

Northerners may think of caladium as a houseplant, but gardeners in the South know better. It is one of the most valuable, lush-growing foliage plants for shade, because it brings a range of bright, attractive color and because it is so easy to grow.

Each plant grows from a small, chubby tuber. The broadly heart-shaped leaves are carried on short stalks. They usually feature dappled patterns accented with solid-color margins and veins, in handsome variations of pink, white, red, and green.

Plantings devoted to one cultivar are breathtaking—try a band of, say, white-and-green ones ribboning under the shade of live oaks. Mixed plantings are equally attractive, perhaps in planters on a porch or in a semishaded eastern or northern exposure. Feeding monthly with an all-purpose fertilizer guarantees a super display.

Caladiums are generally trouble-free, rarely bothered by pests or disease. They thrive in moist, humusy soil and do well in hot, humid summers, but may suffer from rot if the soil doesn't drain well. If you grow them in containers, be sure to attend to the drainage requirement (a hole in the bottom of the pot, and good, rich potting mix). Either way, you'll see that your caladiums slow down in the autumn and go dormant for the winter. If you are at all concerned about their cold-hardiness, simply dig up the dormant tubers and store them for the winter in a cool, dry place indoors.

Caltha palustris

Marsh marigold

HEIGHT/WIDTH: 12"–18" × 9"–12" (30–45cm × 23–30cm)

FLOWERS: yellow buttercups

BLOOM TIME: spring

ZONES: 4–10

Marsh marigold

Damp or wet shade is often difficult to landscape, but your troubles are over—marsh marigold is a splendid candidate for a starring role in such conditions. The succulent, cabbagelike leaves will thrive, and spread by means of runners, until the whole area is covered.

Each spring you will be treated to a short but exuberant flowering show. Marsh marigold flowers really are sensational. They are sunny yellow, about 2 inches (5cm) across, and carried in clusters; they look a great deal like buttercups, to which they are related. A cultivar, 'Plena', has double flowers. Their brightness makes them a pleasant companion for spring bulbs that don't mind similar conditions (such as camas or winter aconite); and, after all the flowers fade, marsh marigold foliage stays around to cover up and carry on.

If your soil begins to dry out as summer advances, the leaves will gradually die down and fade from view and the plant will go dormant. If this leaves you with a bare area, be sure to plant marsh marigold in the company of other things that continue the show, like cardinal flower or irises.

Campanula spp.

Bellflower

HEIGHT/WIDTH: 1'–4' × 6"–2' (30–120cm × 15–60cm)

FLOWERS: blue, purple, pink, or white bells

BLOOM TIME: summer

ZONES: 4–8

Bellflower

Many members of the campanula tribe will do well in some shade, which preserves the flower color. The taller, upright-growing ones are probably best for attracting notice—in dappled, not deep, shade, such as at the edge of a woodland or in a spot that receives some morning sun and is shielded from hot afternoon rays. For the most part, they require moist, well-drained soil that is not acidic.

Among the top choices are great bellflower (*C. latifolia*), clustered bellflower (*C. glomerata*), and milky bellflower (*C. lactiflora*). The first has small racemes of tubular flowers atop thick, unbranched stems that don't require staking. There are some nice cultivars of this one, including handsome white 'Alba', atmospheric 'Gloaming', with pale, smoky blue flowers, and 'Macrantha' (also known as *C. lactiflora* var. *macrantha*), with larger, royal purple blooms.

Clustered bellflower, as the name suggests, carries its funnel-shaped flowers in large, loose clusters. The plant blooms lushly, so it is a good choice where you really want a show. It, too, hosts a number of worthy selections, among them dark periwinkle blue 'Joan Elliot' and the taller 'Superba', as well as white 'Crown of Snow'.

As for milky bellflower, it is a tall plant, sometimes reaching as much as 5 feet (1.5m), and laden with large, heavy panicles that look from a distance like scoops of ice cream. You will have to stake this flower, or set it adjacent to plants it can lean on. The lovely 'Loddon Anna' has soft pink blooms.

Caulophyllum thalictroides

Blue cohosh

HEIGHT/WIDTH: 1'–2' × 6" (30–60cm × 15cm)

FLOWERS: tiny, brownish

BLOOM TIME: spring

ZONES: 3–8

Blue cohosh

Grow this plant for its autumn berries, which are sensational. There is a buildup to get them, but it is always interesting. First, in early spring, the tiny, ½-inch (1.5cm) flowers emerge; they're brownish green to brownish purple with yellow stamens and pistils—not very attractive. Shortly, the small flowers are joined by tufts of dark purple foliage that will remind you of columbines. As the season progresses, the odd flowers fade and the foliage expands and turns deep blue-green, a color match for the leaves of some hostas.

At last, in autumn, the round, peasize berries pop out of the seed capsules. They are green at first, but one day you stop dead in your tracks and gasp at their beauty—they've become magnificent, rich, bright violet-blue. You can't miss them, nor will anyone else who visits your garden at this time of year.

For best results, grow blue cohosh in moist, fertile, acidic soil. Part shade is fine; full shade is too. The plant doesn't tend to spread much, because the seeds embedded in those fabulous berries germinate slowly and erratically.

Centranthus ruber

Red valerian, Jupiter's beard

HEIGHT/WIDTH: 2'–3' × 2'–3' (60–90cm × 60–90cm)

FLOWERS: red or white

BLOOM TIME: summer

ZONES: 5–8

Red valerian

A wanderer at heart, red valerian may begin life in your garden in a sunny border but eventually seed its way into semishady nooks and crannies. No matter where this plant grows, you'll enjoy the remarkably long-lasting, sweetly fragrant blooms, which in the species are rosy crimson. (A white version, 'Albus', is easy to find, and a little hunting in specialty nurseries will turn up the lovely pink-hued 'Roseus'.)

Individual blooms are only about half an inch (1.5cm) across, but the flower heads are dense with them. Butterflies adore these flowers. They also make terrific bouquets.

This adaptable plant is also easygoing about its soil preferences. It doesn't care for extremes of wet or dryness but otherwise will grow just about anywhere. Established plants are quite drought-tolerant, and drier soil also seems to inspire more compact growth. Only very hot, humid summers cause this exuberant plant to flag.

Since valerian is in bloom for practically the whole summer, it is probably best planted solo, so it doesn't steal the show. To vary things a bit, just grow more than one color. You'll notice that the sage green foliage shows up well against the dark background of shrubs and hedges.

Chrysogonum virginianum

Goldenstar, green-and-gold

HEIGHT/WIDTH: 4"–1' × 1'–2' (10–30cm × 30–60cm)

FLOWERS: small yellow daisies

BLOOM TIME: late spring–summer

ZONES: 5–9

Goldenstar

Few other groundcovers for partial shade bloom as brightly and continually as little goldenstar. A low, spreading (but not aggressive) plant, it has dark green, heart-shaped leaves and bears marvelous, glowing yellow, 1½-inch (4cm) daisy-like blooms on short stalks. If you grow it in soil that is neither boggy nor dry, it will bloom generously for many weeks and thereafter produce occasional blooms until cold weather arrives. A cultivar, 'Pierre', is smaller than the species and prized for its especially long bloom period.

A wildflower native to the area from the Appalachians south to Florida, goldenstar will surely thrive in gardens in that part of the United States. But it does just fine further north, provided you give it a good winter mulch.

Mass plantings, as along a woodland walkway or bordering a line of shrubs, always look great and call attention to the vivacious though small flowers. You can successfully combine goldenstar with other flowers—make a lively carpet of color by growing it with columbine or Virginia bluebells.

Cimicifuga racemosa

Bugbane

HEIGHT/WIDTH: 3'–6' × 3' (90–180cm × 90cm)

FLOWERS: white spires

BLOOM TIME: midsummer

ZONES: 3–8

Bugbane

A tall, full plant, bugbane is magnificent in the right setting. It is best employed in back of shorter plants, where its imposing presence enhances rather than overwhelms; some gardeners like to place it in the middle of an "island bed," where it can be admired from all sides. A solo performance under deciduous trees, perhaps with ferns at its feet, is guaranteed to be dramatic.

The dark green, much-divided foliage creates a bushlike form up to about 3 feet (90cm) tall and wide. The creamy white flower plumes, 6 inches (15cm) or longer, rise up an additional 2 or 3 feet (60 or 90cm) above the foliage and are a sight to behold: they are branched, rather than individual, spires, so the effect is like candelabras. Bugbane puts on a regal show for several weeks in midsummer, and never needs propping up. Some nurseries don't mention the scent, while others tell you it's "rank," but the truth is that it's not very obtrusive.

Cimicifuga is long-lived and trouble-free, unfussy about soil and asking only for sufficient moisture. The more shade it receives (although it is not suitable for deep gloom), the longer-lasting those remarkable blooms will be.

Coleus × hybridus

Coleus

HEIGHT/WIDTH: 1'–3' × 1'–3' (30–90cm × 30–90cm)

FLOWERS: purple spires

BLOOM TIME: summer

ZONES: all zones (annual)

'Color Pride' coleus

Although often thought of as a houseplant, coleus can be grown outdoors anywhere the summers are warm—just consider it an annual, and tear it out before cold weather comes. It adapts well to any shady location, even deep, dark shade, provided its soil is moist and well drained (dry soil causes it to become leggy, look increasingly awful, and finally expire).

There are now literally hundreds of crisply colorful varieties on the market, and a bed devoted to coleus alone or in tandem with other foliage plants can be quite an appealing sight. You've probably seen the ones sporting plain red leaves with green borders everywhere, but there are also some unusual beauties, such as ones with eggshell white, claret red, or gold-bronze interiors and lighter or richer green borders or veination. Some of the new dwarf varieties don't need any pinching to grow naturally bushy.

A word to the wise about finding these interesting coleus selections: shop for seeds. Most large seed companies offer several intriguing choices, and coleus is a cinch to grow from seed.

Comptonia peregrina

Sweetfern

HEIGHT/WIDTH: 2'–4' (60–120cm)/spreading habit

FLOWERS: tiny yellow-green catkins

BLOOM TIME: summer

ZONES: 4–7

Sweetfern

Not a fern at all, but rather a deciduous shrub with lush, aromatic foliage and inconspicuous flowers, sweetfern is prized for its ability to tolerate difficult conditions. It grows in sandy, acidic, infertile soil in the wild, and tolerates the abuses of wind, weather, and even pollution. It is rarely bothered by any pests or diseases, and unlike some shrubby plants, it requires little pruning to remain the same height.

Once established, however, sweetfern will not stay within its bounds to the sides. Its species name, *peregrina*, refers to the fact that it "peregrinates," or wanders and spreads at will. So it would be an appropriate choice for landscaping a partially shaded, naturalistic area with poor soil. It is one of the few plants able to tolerate seaside areas with aplomb.

The long, lance-shaped leaves more or less resemble skinny fern leaves, though they are mostly carried in loose clusters that give the plant a carefree profile. They are dark green above and lighter below. On hot days, or when you rub your hands on them, they radiate an enchanting spicy-fern fragrance

The only thing that has kept this fine plant from being grown more widely is the difficulties of propagating and transplanting it. Fortunately, some nurseries have succeeded in raising some from root cuttings, and you should look for these and plant them while they're young.

Convallaria majalis

Lily-of-the-valley

HEIGHT/WIDTH: 4"–8" × 8"–12" (10–20cm × 20–30cm)

FLOWERS: tiny white bells

BLOOM TIME: late spring

ZONES: 2–9

Lily-of-the-valley

Ah, what would springtime be like without the gentle, romantic scent of lily-of-the-valley wafting across the yard? When it has the right conditions—humusy soil and part to full shade—this old favorite makes a superb groundcover, blanketing broad areas with its glossy lilylike foliage and excluding weeds.

The deliciously fragrant small bells line separate stems that rise above the carpet of green leaves. They have a waxy texture, which helps them tolerate the vagaries of springtime weather, allows them to last many weeks in the ground, and makes it possible for them to transfer with grace to a petite vase indoors.

Much as you may adore the original species, some of the newer cultivars are worth considering. 'Albostriata' has white-striped leaves that are very attractive. Larger-flowered cultivars also are available, including 'Fortin's Giant' and the double-flowered 'Flore Pleno'. The one with pale pink bells may also win your heart (it's called var. *rosea*). Any of these are worth growing on their own or mixing together. Note that lily-of-the-valley is sold as "pips," which are simply pieces of fleshy rhizome. Don't let them dry out—plant them immediately upon arrival at your home, or soak them in a bowl of water until you're ready. Hopefully, they will flower their first year.

Cornus canadensis

Bunchberry

HEIGHT/WIDTH: 3"–9" (7.5–23cm)/spreading habit

FLOWERS: white

BLOOM TIME: spring

ZONES: 2–6

Bunchberry

In its native woods, bunchberry grows in broad colonies, lighting up the gloom with its large (for the plant's size) white flowers—a sight you can imitate in your garden. It must have humus-rich, moist, well-drained soil to do well, however, so it is happiest under deciduous trees or a combination of deciduous and evergreen ones (the ground under a grove of shallow-rooted evergreens is often too dry and infertile). It is also nice at the feet of acid-soil-loving shrubs such as rhododendrons and azaleas.

The flowers look just like dogwood-tree flowers, or rather "bracts," which is no surprise, as this plant is the same species. The orange-red berries that follow by autumn are also characteristic and, while pulpy to our taste, are beloved by birds. As for the leaves, they grow in a loose whorl around the stem and are a nice, shiny green. In sheltered locations, they may last all winter.

Some gardeners have had trouble establishing bunchberry, so here are a few tips to ensure success. Obviously, the site should be suitable, as described above. Your best bet is to start with young seedlings; although bunchberry can be grown from seed, this is a tedious process best left to the nursery. Also, older plants tend to be woodier and resent transplanting. Keep your crop well watered its first season, and add a moisture-retaining mulch. If your plants are happy, over the years they will spread far and wide throughout your shade garden; extras are easily removed.

Corydalis lutea

Golden corydalis

HEIGHT/WIDTH: 12"–16" × 12" (30–40.5cm × 30cm)

FLOWERS: yellow

BLOOM TIME: spring–autumn

ZONES: 4–8

Golden corydalis

A champion for cool, moist soil in partial shade, golden corydalis blooms heartily all summer long. Its small, tubular, rich yellow flowers are held aloft in lush racemes. At season's end, they shed plenty of seeds. Let them—new plants will turn up in unexpected places (even hugging a stone wall!). A border, pathside, or woodland turned over to them is always a cheerful sight, especially on gray days.

The plant forms a low mound of lacy, ferny foliage that looks very much like bleeding heart foliage (the two plants are not related, however). It is evergreen, though in the northern reaches of its range winter protection is advisable.

In recent years, fabulous blue-flowered versions of this plant have appeared in North America and Europe; they hail from China's Sichuan province. The most popular of the blue-flowered cultivars is electric blue 'Blue Panda', which blooms over just as long a period as golden corydalis, if not longer. While 'Blue Panda' tolerates light shade, less sun tends to make it grow a bit leggy.

Cyclamen hederifolium

Ivy-leaved cyclamen, baby cyclamen

HEIGHT/WIDTH: 3"–5" × 5"–8" (7.5–13cm × 13–20cm)

FLOWERS: pink or white

BLOOM TIME: autumn

ZONES: 5–9

Ivy-leaved cyclamen

Gardeners who fancy late-flowering bulbous plants agree, this hardy cyclamen is the prettiest of them all. The flowers look just like those of the florist cyclamen, its cousin, they are just much smaller, about an inch (2.5cm) across. Perched atop graceful, bare stems, they are usually pink and sometimes white, and a patch of them in bloom, with all their swept-back petals, is a truly enchanting sight.

But perhaps the greatest attraction of ivy-leaved cyclamen is its magnificent foliage. Each individual leaf is a study in light and dark green, with silver highlights and purplish-green undersides. Occasionally you'll notice an all-green one, or an almost entirely silver one, but this variability just enhances the value of the plant as a beautiful groundcover.

Like all cyclamen, it grows from a stout little tuber. Plant it in the spring, shallowly, in ground that is loamy and well drained. The high shade under deciduous trees is ideal. Ivy-leaved cyclamen is a tough little customer; it will manage to thrive in dry shade and survive hot, dry summers by going dormant. When conditions are right, the plant self-sows freely, enlarging the size of the patch you've now become so enamored of.

Darmera peltata

(Peltiphyllum peltatum)

Umbrella plant

HEIGHT/WIDTH: 3'–6' × 2'–3' (90–180cm × 60–90cm)

FLOWERS: pink flower heads

BLOOM TIME: spring

ZONES: 5–9

Umbrella plant

Want a bold plant in your semishady garden, bolder than the broadest-leaved hosta? Try umbrella plant, which earns its name from its tall stems bearing large, prominently veined, spreading leaves, a foot or two (30 or 60cm) across. You almost expect a mischievous troll or hobbit to appear under their shelter. For today's smaller gardens, this plant is certainly a realistic alternative to the massive *Gunnera manicata*, which has a similar form but is easily twice as large—and not as hardy.

The first, and probably only, requirement for success with this handsome plant is moist soil. In nature, it is found along streams and pond edges. It tolerates periods of standing water, so you could put it in a boggy area that tends to dry up a bit as summer progresses. It also prospers in heavy clay soil, where few other things will grow.

The flowers precede the leaves in early spring. They are borne on tall leafless stems and are bright to lilac pink, occasionally pinkish white. They are fleeting, but pretty while they last.

At season's end, the gardener gets another treat, particularly if the summer has been mild. The leaves turn a flaming coppery orange-red, highlighted with yellow veins.

Dicentra spectabilis

Bleeding heart

HEIGHT/WIDTH: 2'–3' × 2' (60–90cm × 60cm)

FLOWERS: pink-and-white

BLOOM TIME: spring

ZONES: 3–9

'Alba' bleeding heart

This beloved plant is a shade garden classic, with good reason. It has truly stood the test of time, with no need for improvement by plant breeders. It looks terrific solo, in a spot where it has adequate elbowroom. It's also nice massed under shade trees or on the north or east side of a house or garage, though it's too tall and full to be considered a groundcover per se. Another favorite use for it is among spring-flowering bulbs or wildflowers, because it comes on a bit later, taking over the show just as the other plants begin to flag, and covering up or distracting from dying foliage. Moist soil is required for bleeding heart to prosper.

The plant's ferny, much-divided foliage forms a beautiful, loose mound about as wide as it is tall, and the endearing, 1-inch (2.5cm) locket-shaped flowers line arching stems. The plain species is pink-and-white flowered. A cultivar, 'Alba', has all-white blooms, and is not quite as vigorous a grower. Both will stay in bloom for as long as six weeks, provided your spring weather is not too capricious. Afterward, the attractive foliage remains and holds its own pretty well for the rest of the season; in warmer areas or drier soils, however, it may simply throw in the towel and go dormant by midsummer.

Digitalis grandiflora
(*D. ambigua*)

Yellow foxglove

HEIGHT/WIDTH: 2'–3' × 1'–2' (60–90cm × 30–60cm)

FLOWERS: yellow bells

BLOOM TIME: summer

ZONES: 3–8

Yellow foxglove

This pretty foxglove not only is perennial (unlike many of its relatives), but also blooms over many weeks each summer. Shade becomes it, preserving the longevity of the flowers and highlighting their soft, appealing glow.

This one is not as formal-looking as some of its kin. Its growth is shaggier and it always produces lots of lopsided flower spikes. While the color is subtle enough to mix with other shade-tolerant bloomers—imagine it among yellow-rimmed hostas or at a woodland's edge with red cardinal flower or poppies—perhaps its best use is its natural inclination. Yellow foxglove doesn't just return year after year, it also spills its seeds to generate more plants. Let it naturalize.

Close inspection reveals that the flowers are dotted and striped inside with chocolate brown. Bring them indoors for bouquets so everyone can admire them—just remember to pick early, when they're half open, for best results.

Disporum spp.

Fairybells

HEIGHT/WIDTH: 2'–3' × 1' (60–90cm × 30cm)

FLOWERS: white or yellow bells

BLOOM TIME: early spring

ZONES: 4–9

Fairybells

Sometimes wonderful woodland plants come from unexpected places. In recent years, plant explorers have found a bonanza of garden-worthy ones in Korea and Japan, and these introductions have made their way into specialty plant catalogs and nurseries. One such prize is a number of new fairybells.

If you've encountered fairybells at all, you've most likely seen the broad-leaved *D. sessile* 'Variegatum', which has liberally striped foliage that makes a splash in shady places. With oblong or lance-shaped foliage lining the stems, this plant is superficially similar to Solomon's seal. The 1-inch (2.5cm) pendant, tubular flowers, however, are carried on their own stalks, in pairs or clusters. In the case of 'Variegatum', they're off-white. Those of the less common but equally enchanting *D. flavens* are soft yellow (the foliage is shiny green). In autumn, the flowers yield to blue-black berries. The green-leaved *D. hookeri* has greenish bells and orange-red berries.

A spreading clump-former, this amiable plant has a lot going for it. The shiny, heavy-textured leaves are quite attractive and keep up appearances even in dry shade. The only potential problems, slugs and leaf-disfiguring fungi, may be kept at bay if fairybells is grown in well-drained soil.

Dryopteris marginalis

Wood fern, marginal shield fern

HEIGHT/WIDTH: 2'–3' × 1'–2' (60–90cm × 30–60cm)

FLOWERS: (not a flowering plant)

BLOOM TIME: (not applicable)

ZONES: 3–8

Wood fern

For many people, this is the ideal fern. The fronds are dark blue-green, are neat and uniform, and have a crisp texture. Wood fern is popular with florists, who prize it as handsome, long-lasting greenery to embellish bouquets, and you can certainly harvest your homegrown fronds for the same use. Because it is shorter than some other garden-worthy ferns, and because it doesn't tend to spread much, wood fern is a nice choice for mixing with flowering plants without over-whelming or overarching them. Celandine poppy and foam-flower are two suitable companions.

In the wild, wood fern grows on rocky woodland slopes, which hints at its most critical need besides shade: well-drained soil. It does not appear to be particular about soil pH, tolerating both acidic and alkaline spots equally well. Moisture, though, is key. If your wooded area dries out in the summer months, help your ferns along with a lit-tle extra moisture and/or mulch. In milder climates, wood fern is evergreen over the winter. Elsewhere, you'll look forward to fiddleheads announcing this fern's revival each spring.

Epimedium spp.

Epimedium, bishop's-hat, barrenwort

HEIGHT/WIDTH: 6"–1' × 1'–2' (15–30cm × 30–60cm)

FLOWERS: small clusters; color varies

BLOOM TIME: spring

ZONES: 4–8

Red epimedium

Here is a plant that looks delicate but is tough and versatile. It will grow equally well in damp or dry shade. It does well carpeting the ground under trees and shrubs, seemingly untroubled by the competition. It also makes a good-looking edging along a shady garden path. Epimedium's only drawback is that it is not a fast increaser, so you should plant individuals fairly close together, say, a foot (30cm) apart.

Generally speaking, these plants have pretty, oblong-heart-shaped leaflets on wiry stems. The leaves are red or bronze when they emerge in early spring, change to red- or chocolate-tinged green over the course of the summer, and may also be rimmed in red. Some are evergreen over the winter, some are not, so if this characteristic matters to you, ask the nursery before you buy.

The spurred flowers, which appear for a brief but generous display in spring, are small, borne in clusters, and vary from white to yellow to bright pink to scarlet, sometimes with contrasting spurs of white or yellow. They are not the prime reason to grow the plant, and in some species they are even hidden by the foliage.

Some choice epimediums to look for include red epimedium (*E. × rubrum*), which has contrasting bicolor red or pink and white blooms; yellow-flowered, lime green–leaved Persian epimedium (*E. × versicolor* 'Sulphureum'); and the smaller, green-leaved *E. youngianum* cultivars ('Niveum' has white flowers, 'Roseum' has pink ones).

Erythronium spp.

Trout lily, fawn lily

HEIGHT/WIDTH: 5"–12" × 5"–12" (13–30cm × 13–30cm)

FLOWERS: yellow, white, or pink

BLOOM TIME: spring

ZONES: 4–8

'Pagoda' trout lily

The best place for this appealing native wildflower is high, open shade under deciduous trees. The soil should be organically rich and well drained. There, your trout lilies will thrive and multiply, filling your woodland with beauty each spring.

Trout lilies probably get their whimsical name from their distinctive foliage; each plant sports just two simple, lance-shaped leaves, mottled or speckled with brown, purple, or even cream markings. One botanist suggests that the other common name, "fawn lily," is inspired by their resemblance to the perked-up ears of a young deer.

The bloom rises above the pair of leaves on a slender, wiry stem. It's a pretty thing, between 1 and 3 inches (2.5 and 7.5cm) across and looking very much like a nodding, slightly flared lily flower (the plant is in the same family as cultivated lilies). The flowers of *E. americanum* are chiffon yellow brushed with chocolate brown marks. Because those of the enchanting *E. revolutum* vary from rosy pink to soft pink to white, selections were inevitable. 'Rose Beauty' and 'White Beauty' are available from bulb suppliers and specialty nurseries.

But perhaps the most popular cultivar, apparently derived from *E. tuolumnense*, is the sunny yellow 'Pagoda'. Its flowers and leaves are much larger than those of the others, and it is an eager, robust grower. A patch of these makes a marvelously cheery golden carpet over the dull brown ground of early spring.

Euonymus fortunei

Wintercreeper

HEIGHT/WIDTH: 4"–6" (10–15cm)/spreading habit

FLOWERS: inconspicuous; greenish white

BLOOM TIME: early summer

ZONES: 5–9

'Emerald Gaiety' wintercreeper

You know this plant—it is that tough-leaved, fast-growing, spreading vine, low shrub, or groundcover. It has been extensively hybridized, perhaps too much so, as some cultivars are rather similar to others. Many are variegated, which accounts for the plant's enduring appeal in part to full shade. 'Variegata' or 'Variegated' may have white or yellow markings or margins. 'Silver Queen' has pronounced white edges. Compact-growing 'Emerald Gaiety' is generally viewed as one of the best, with rounded green leaves that are liberally rimmed in white; these turn reddish in colder weather. Still another popular one is 'Colorata' (or var. *coloratus*), which has a plum-purple color in autumn and winter. Others have brighter, splashier yellow-and-green variegation, larger leaves, smaller leaves, and so on. All are tolerant of most soils (except downright boggy conditions).

Opinions on this overused plant vary. The accomplished gardener and author Sydney Eddison, who grows 'Emerald Gaiety' in her Connecticut garden, gratefully calls it "a godsend" because it not only survives but also thrives in a difficult site among rocks and tangled tree roots. Meanwhile, the ornamental plant expert Michael Dirr can barely contain his scorn, saying: "From seventeen feet [5m] away, [the cultivars] all look the same." Given its fast growth and rather coarse appearance, this euonymus is probably best used where nothing else does well.

Eupatorium coelestinum

Mist flower

HEIGHT/WIDTH: 1'–3' × 1'–2' (30–90cm × 30–60cm)

FLOWERS: small purple heads

BLOOM TIME: late summer–autumn

ZONES: 5–10

Mist flower

If you are careful with the siting of this pretty, late-blooming plant, you will be more than delighted with its performance. A naturally rampant grower in damp soils, it becomes perfectly manageable in dry shade. If you must grow it in moist ground, you can control its spread by occasionally digging out and discarding or giving away unwanted offspring. Another trick is to cut the plant low in early summer. It will rebound but be of more compact habit, and still bloom at the usual time.

Mist flower's late summer to early autumn bloom period is a real asset, especially since the flowers are so long-lasting—up to eight weeks! They look quite a bit like the familiar annual ageratum, with profuse, flattened flower heads in blue or lilac. But individual blossoms are fluffier and more spidery. Also, the fact that they are borne on a taller plant, not a groundcovering bedding plant, means that you can enjoy them in semiwild borders or woodland edges. They also make pretty cut flowers.

The cultivar 'Wayside' is available from Wayside Gardens. It is virtually the same as the species, but shorter-growing, to only 2 feet (60cm), which might tempt you to include it in a more controlled border situation.

Galium odoratum

Sweet woodruff

HEIGHT/WIDTH: 6"–1' × 1' (15–30cm × 30cm)

FLOWERS: white stars

BLOOM TIME: spring

ZONES: 3–9

Sweet woodruff

Shade gardeners have long cherished this plant, and it is easy to see why. It is a charmer, from its long, thin, apple green leaves (which occur in whorls along the slender stems) to its small, dainty white flowers. The name refers to the fact that the entire plant exudes a sweet, spicy scent when dried—some people have likened it to vanilla. Craftspeople like to add clumps to the stuffing in pillows and mattresses, and sweet woodruff also has been used to flavor homemade wine.

Easygoing to a fault, this plant will take to almost any soil and spread slowly but surely. Moist soil inspires faster growth. Sweet woodruff is ideal for banks, along pathways, under trees, or as an edging. It is durable enough to withstand some foot traffic or the occasional wayward soccer ball, so some gardeners use it in shady curb-strip plantings and even in the gaps between walkway stones. No matter where you grow sweet woodruff, "volunteers" that appear beyond their bounds are easily pulled out.

Gaultheria procumbens

Wintergreen, checkerberry

HEIGHT/WIDTH: 4"–6" (10–15cm)/spreading habit

FLOWERS: tiny white bells

BLOOM TIME: spring

ZONES: 4–8

Wintergreen

For the longest time, this native North American woodlander was appreciated mainly as a medicinal and culinary herb. The leaves, particularly when bruised or chewed, emit an invigorating menthol scent. The oil, which may be extracted with a lot of time and effort, was used in cough and cold remedies, chewing gum, salves for sore muscles, and even real root beer. It has been upstaged by synthetic imitations or the more easily extracted oil from black birch trees (*Betula lenta*).

Useful or not, wintergreen certainly makes a nice groundcover, preferably under the high shade of deciduous trees—it likes humusy, acidic soil. The small, 1 to 2-inch (2.5 to 5cm) roundish leaves form an attractive, glossy green, somewhat shrubby mat. The tiny, nodding white bell flowers are attractive while they last. And when the round, bright red berries appear, wintergreen looks downright festive. Often both leaves and berries persist over the winter months.

Wintergreen has a creeping rootstock, and self-sows as well. So a few plants ought to become a nice colony after a few seasons.

Gaylussacia brachycera

Box huckleberry

HEIGHT/WIDTH: 6"–18" (15–45cm)/spreading habit

FLOWERS: tiny white or pinkish bells

BLOOM TIME: late spring

ZONES: 5–7

Box huckleberry

You want a groundcover in your rhododendron or azalea patch or at the base of some pine trees, but nothing seems to grow well there. Your search is over: box huckleberry adores such shady, acidic-soil conditions.

Once established, this attractive evergreen will spread its glossy foliage slowly but surely to form a glorious mat of dark green. The flowers, though small, are pretty while they last. These are followed in late summer by tiny bluish berries (technically drupes) that look like blueberries and, while edible, are full of crunchy seeds. In the cold months, the leaves take on a rich bronze or wine-red hue.

This plant has an interesting legend attached to it. Apparently, there is a massive, mile-long patch in central Pennsylvania that is said to have originated from a single plant thousands of years ago. If you grow it, you will observe firsthand its spreading habit. True or not, the story does give testimony to box huckleberry's incredible durability!

Geranium spp.

Cranesbill geranium

HEIGHT/WIDTH: 1'–2' × 1'–2' (30–60cm × 30–60cm)

FLOWERS: many colors

BLOOM TIME: varies

ZONES: 5–9

'Johnson's Blue' cranesbill geranium

Pretty flowers and a long bloom period recommend this group highly to anyone who desires color in their shade garden. Cranesbills look wonderful massed (which makes a virtue out of their mounding or sprawling habits); lower-growing ones can even be used as groundcovers. They thrive in good, not overly rich, soil.

The saucer-shaped flowers come in a range of colors from white to pink to blue, and the dainty petals often have darker-colored veining. The leaves are usually palm-shaped and deeply lobed or cut, and may turn red in autumn, adding a welcome late splash of color when you least expect it.

Perhaps the most popular cranesbill geranium is a hybrid called 'Johnson's Blue'. It produces loads of vivid blue, 2-inch (5cm)-wide flowers. Another choice selection is the lovely and vigorous *G. endressi* 'Wargrave Pink'; the 1-inch (2.5cm) blooms are bright pink. *G. sanguineum* 'Album', a lower-growing type, has pure white 1½-inch (4cm) flowers against a backdrop of dark green leaves.

There are many, many other choices—feast your eyes on the selections at any good perennials nursery, local or mail-order, and treat yourself to a few lovely cranesbill geraniums.

Hakonechloa macra 'Aureola'

Hakonechloa, wind-combed grass

HEIGHT/WIDTH: 6"–18" × 6"–18" (15–45cm ×

15–45cm)

FLOWERS: tiny, pale green spikelets (not grown

for flowers)

BLOOM TIME: late summer

ZONES: 5–9

'Aureola' hakonechloa

Ornamental grasses have been in vogue for a while now, and some of them tolerate less than full sun. But, one might argue, does the shade garden need more foliage plants? If you feel this way, you still ought to consider making an exception for this plant. Hakonechloa, of Japanese origins, is an unusual and unusually beautiful grass.

The long, tapering leaves display a golden glow from a distance. Up close, they are more complex: they are a fine shade of yellow or off-white, generously striped with rich green that contains hints of bronze. (The flowers are incon-

spicuous.) Hakonechloa is deciduous, but before it closes down for the winter, its foliage turns reddish, then soft tan.

The plant has a graceful, low-growing habit that arches and spills over itself like a waterfall. It spreads slowly by means of creeping rhizomes, but if expansion is not your wish, simply rein it in by planting it in a container that is sunk into the ground. A whiskey barrel of it in a shady corner or courtyard would be fabulous. It must have fertile, evenly moist soil that is slightly acidic.

Hedera helix

English ivy

HEIGHT/WIDTH: climbing vine or sprawling groundcover

FLOWERS: tiny, yellowish green (rarely appear)

BLOOM TIME: autumn

ZONES: 5–9

English ivy

If you still think of English ivy as a plain, congested groundcover or "tree eater," it's time for a fresh look. It's true that the broadly heart-shaped leaves of the species are not terribly distinctive (though if you simply want a wall or fence covered, you may still resort to planting it). But nowadays there are dozens of intriguing alternatives.

Perhaps the most exciting new cultivars are the ones with variegated leaves; note that they do prefer a bit more light. 'Adam' has beautiful sage green leaves rimmed and marked with creamy white. 'Calico' leaves are mainly white, bordered in rich green. The bizarre 'Harrison' has smoldering dark leaves defined with white veination; in cold weather, they turn royal purple—a breathtaking sight.

Ivy leaves that are bred to be yellow are also in vogue. 'Sulphur Heart' and 'Gold Heart' have golden interiors. 'Buttercup' has an almost entirely yellow leaf.

You will also find ivies with unusual leaves. 'Curlytop' has fairly full leaves, but they are whimsically curly. 'Fan' has spreading foliage with scalloped edges. These and others bring unexpected texture to your garden.

Consult mail-order catalogs, which offer the best selections, and you may get the best of both worlds—a vigorous, climber with surprising beauty. Remember that most ivies are self-clinging and will attach themselves to fences, walls, trellises, and tree trunks with little help from you.

Helleborus spp.

Hellebore, Lenten rose, Christmas rose

HEIGHT/WIDTH: 2' × 2' (60cm × 60cm)

FLOWERS: color varies

BLOOM TIME: early spring

ZONES: 4–8

Lenten rose

These exquisite flowers are among the earliest signs of life each spring, an unorthodox alternative to all the spring bulbs. Their nodding blooms are sometimes carried singly, sometimes in clusters. Slightly cup-shaped, up to 4 inches (10cm) across, they come in shades of pristine white, cream, lime green, pink, rose, lavender, purple, even blue-black. The lighter-colored ones are often blushed, speckled, or edged with a darker hue. All are centered with a boss of dainty yellow stamens. At first glance, hellebores are reminiscent of single-form roses—hence the common names. The attractive leaves are carried in compound leaflets, and may be evergreen if your winters are not too harsh.

The hellebores you are most likely to find in nurseries are Christmas rose (*H. niger*), which can be tricky to grow well, and the smaller-flowered Lenten rose (*H. orientalis*). The so-called stinking hellebore (*H. foetidus*) actually only releases its scent if bruised, and it's really not that offensive; the flowers are enchanting green bells edged with purple-red.

Named cultivars are hard to come by, but there's nothing wrong with planting some seed-grown ones in a shady spot and waiting to see what blooms. Pamper them by making sure their soil is cool, moist, and slightly alkaline. It should also be very fertile, with plenty of organic material; provide top-dressings at least once a season as well.

Heuchera spp.

Coralbells, alumroot

HEIGHT/WIDTH: 1'–3' × 1'–2' (30–90cm × 30–60cm)

FLOWERS: delicate bells; pink, red, or white

BLOOM TIME: spring–summer

ZONES: 3–9

Coralbells

You can have it all with these shade lovers: stunning foliage and attractive flowers. The durable leaves are produced in mannerly clumps, and look a bit like those of ivy, though more rounded. They remain good-looking all season long, making the plant an ideal choice for a semishady perennial border or even a naturalized groundcover.

Recent years have seen a flurry of new introductions featuring gorgeous foliage variations (frequently a result of breeding with various closely related species). The popular 'Palace Purple' features rich, maroon to royal purple leaves. Other selections are bronze, russet, or silvery, or have these colors on their veins only for a rich, tapestrylike appearance.

The names are mouthwatering: 'Cappuccino', 'Cathedral Windows', 'Chocolate Ruffles', 'Plum Pudding', 'Velvet Night'.

Certain hybrids are treasured for their petite but splendid flowers, arrayed along tall, graceful stalks above the leaves in spring or early summer. These remain in bloom for several weeks, and can even be used as cut flowers. 'Mt. St. Helens' has glowing red flowers, 'Coral Cloud' has pinkish coral flowers, and there are a few white-flowered selections ('June Bride', 'White Cloud'). Planted in groups, coralbells in bloom brings an enchanting, fairyland quality to the shady garden.

Hosta spp.

Hosta, plantain lily

HEIGHT/WIDTH: varies

FLOWERS: white or lavender

BLOOM TIME: varies

ZONES: 3–9

Hosta

Admittedly, hostas are a shade garden cliche, but before you decide to do without them, take a look at the offerings in a specialty nursery catalog or at a well-stocked perennials nursery. You will be amazed at the variation, and may be tempted to create a planting that uses several different ones for a richly hued, many-textured carpet. Certain ones also make excellent accent plants. In any case, for a sterling performance, plant your hostas in dappled shade, in cool soil that is fertile and moist.

When shopping for hostas, consider size first: there are small, mounding types that stay less than a foot (30cm) across as well as great broad-shouldered ones that spread out at maturity to almost 3 feet (90cm) across. There is also great diversity in leaf color, perhaps more so than with any other foliage plant, from a soft blue-green to a bright minty green. Many have leaves that are white- or gold-rimmed or marked with light green variegation. And last but not least, there is texture—some hosta leaves are sleek, some are ribbed or quilted, and some are quite puckered.

Although hosta's greatest value is as a foliage plant, don't overlook its flowers, which come in either white or lavender. These line arching stalks and appear from late spring to late summer, depending on the variety. They can be quite a show in their own right, especially planted in a grouping.

Houttuynia cordata 'Chameleon'

Houttuynia, chameleon plant

HEIGHT/WIDTH: 6"–12" (15–30cm)/spreading habit

FLOWERS: white

BLOOM TIME: early summer

ZONES: 4–9

'Chameleon' houttuynia

If you seek a multicolored, low-growing carpeter for your shade garden, there is no finer plant than this. The heart-shaped green leaves are liberally splashed with cream and pink or red, no two alike. So a patch is a picture in varying hues. This plant is particularly welcome in deep gloom, where few other plants thrive.

The flowers, when they appear, are nothing to write home about. They're only half an inch to an inch (1.5 to 2.5cm) across, and consist of a prominent little white spike and four small white bracts ("petals").

Houttuynia loves moist soil and greedily spreads far and wide in such a setting, given half a chance. It can even grow in shallow, standing water, as at a streamside or bordering—or even wading into—a pool. Ground that is drier seems to rein it in a bit. But if you find it wandering where it shouldn't, simply mow off or tug out unwanted sections.

Allegedly, there are other cultivars of this plant, but the situation appears to be confused, though whether the fault lies with the nurseries or the botanists is unclear. 'Tricolor' is virtually indistinguishable from 'Chameleon'.

Impatiens walleriana

Impatiens, busy Lizzie

HEIGHT/WIDTH: 1'–2' × 1'–2' (30–60cm × 30–60cm)

FLOWERS: color varies

BLOOM TIME: summer

ZONES: grown as an annual

'Super Elfin Twilight' impatiens

Few plants are as utterly dependable in shade as impatiens. They are simply remarkable performers, never failing to pump out a constant supply of neat flowers week after week, month after month, in all but the heaviest shade. The lance-shaped foliage, which varies from light to dark green, is reliably attractive. (The original, red-flowered species from which the many modern hybrids are derived is a tender perennial native to tropical Africa, where it prospers on the forest floor.)

Recent years have seen an explosion of terrific new impatiens, generally in "series," meaning you can buy mixed seed packets or seek out specific colors or color combinations in the bedding plant section of your local nursery. The superb Super Elfin series, as the name suggests, is a group of compact-growing plants, and the color range is wide: every pastel imaginable, as well as more vivid hues of orange, pink, red, and violet-purple. There are also bicolor impatiens, and ones with a central white star or eye. And there is still a lot to be said for planting plain white ones; a ribbon of these through a dim area under oaks or other shade trees never fails to brighten the scene.

Note that the New Guinea impatiens group, with its variegated leaves and larger flowers, can take more sun. However, in especially long, hot summers, impatiens of all kinds must have shelter from the sun.

Imperata cylindrica 'Rubra'

Japanese blood grass

HEIGHT/WIDTH: 1'–2' × 1'–2' (30–60cm × 30–60cm)

FLOWERS: short, silvery spikelets

BLOOM TIME: summer

ZONES: 5–9

Japanese blood grass

Grasses are an unorthodox choice for a shade garden, but there are a few that do just fine in limited light. Japanese blood grass is one. The long, casually upright, flat blades are not uniformly red; instead, the bases are greenish and the color gradually segues to increasingly intense crimson at the tips. The effect is like a small bonfire.

In a smaller garden, a mature plant makes a fabulous accent plant. When Japanese blood grass is grown en masse, of course, its sensational beauty is magnified—but you had better have the space to devote to it, because it will be a scene-stealer.

You often see Japanese blood grass photographed backlit, which dramatizes the glow. You won't get this effect in your garden if you site one or more plants behind others, of course. Better, then, to place it in a more open setting, where shade is light or filtered, perhaps in a west- or east-facing bed or along a pathway. Wherever you grow it, be sure the soil is moist but well drained.

This grass is not as tall or vigorous as some others, and spreads slowly over the years by means of creeping rhizomes. Also, it is rarely troubled by any insect pests or diseases, so, overall, you may find it quite easygoing.

Iris cristata

Dwarf crested iris

HEIGHT/WIDTH: 4"–12" × 2"–4" (10–30cm × 5–10cm)

FLOWERS: small iris, usually lavender

BLOOM TIME: spring

ZONES: 4–8

'Summer Storm' dwarf crested iris

It is true, almost any iris can be grown in partial shade, but do you want to expend the large, magnificent beardeds and Louisianas and the classically beautiful Siberians and Japanese this way? Better to let them take their glory out in the sun—and turn the shade over to this diminutive but utterly enchanting species.

Crested iris is shade tolerant, and it prefers lean, well-drained, even dry soils. Be sure to plant the fleshy roots very near the surface. Then, sit back. Don't fertilize, and don't water except during periods of drought. Over the years, if it is happy, it will form a dense patch. You will also be pleased to learn that this iris is not attacked by the dreaded iris borer, which can devastate its fancy cultivated relatives.

Its lightly scented flowers may be small, but they display plenty of perky color. Petals are marked with royal purple and lavender; the "crest" is yellow and white. (There is also a rare and lovely 'Alba', which is white with a golden crest.) Bladelike, light green leaves carry on the show after the blooms pass; their little tufts, growing en masse, make an attractive groundcover. Alternatively, crested iris is a terrific addition to a semishady rock garden.

Kirengshoma
palmata

Kirengshoma

HEIGHT/WIDTH: 2'–4' × 2'–3' (60–120cm × 60–90cm)

FLOWERS: yellow bells

BLOOM TIME: late summer

ZONES: 5–9

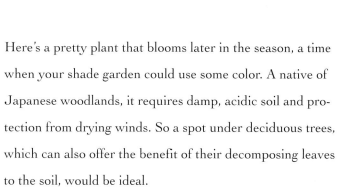

Kirengshoma

Here's a pretty plant that blooms later in the season, a time when your shade garden could use some color. A native of Japanese woodlands, it requires damp, acidic soil and protection from drying winds. So a spot under deciduous trees, which can also offer the benefit of their decomposing leaves to the soil, would be ideal.

Kirengshoma is a rather tall, multistemmed plant, so it should be grown in small groups or toward the back of a shade border. Its arching stems, which are dark red or purple, display pairs of maplelike leaves that get smaller as they ascend. So it is a striking plant, even when not in bloom.

When they finally debut, the flowers are lovely things, little drooping, butter yellow, tubular bells, somewhat reminiscent of campanula blooms. They are carried in threes, generally, which helps them to stand out, for individually they are only between 1 and 2 inches (2.5 and 5cm) long. The blooms last for many weeks, so the wait is well worth it.

Lamiastrum galeobdolon

Lamiastrum, golden dead nettle, yellow archangel

HEIGHT/WIDTH: 1'–2'/spreading (30–60cm/spreading)

FLOWERS: yellow

BLOOM TIME: spring

ZONES: 3–9

'Herman's Pride' lamiastrum

An attractive, spreading choice for dry shade, lamiastrum is closely related to the more common lamium. Like lamium, its leaves are opposite and rather heart-shaped; they may be mint green or variegated with silver or pewter. Individual plants are mounding and spread quickly in the right conditions: semishade and decent soil. The upside is that lamiastrum naturally forms nice, uniform patches that have a tidy demeanor, so a glade devoted to this plant need not look out of control or unkempt. To further exercise control, you can cut the plant back after flowering.

The springtime flowers are a tempting reason to grow this plant. The cultivar you usually see, 'Herman's Pride', is spangled with dense clusters of golden yellow flowers (a color you won't see in lamium, and a main reason this plant was separated off from that genus). The flowers in conjunction with the silver-flecked foliage make a vivacious show.

Lamium maculatum

Lamium, spotted dead nettle

HEIGHT/WIDTH: 1'–2' × 1' (30–60cm × 30cm)

FLOWERS: small clusters; white or pink

BLOOM TIME: summer

ZONES: 4–8

'White Nancy' lamium

Especially good-looking variegated foliage is the reason to invite this justly popular groundcover into your shade garden. The oval leaves are a fresh green, spotted, ribbed, or marked with white, light green, or silver. 'White Nancy' and 'Beacon Silver', the most commonly seen cultivars, have green-rimmed foliage that is otherwise entirely silver. The newer, luscious 'Chequers' has heavily marbled leaves; the background is rich red, and the veins are silvery.

A nice plus about these plants is their flowers, which nearly steal the show when they appear for several weeks each summer. Each is less than an inch (2.5cm) long, with a hooded shape. The flowers are borne in tight little clusters that stand slightly above the foliage. Those of the aforementioned 'White Nancy' are white, which in combination with the leaves really make the plants "pop" out of the shade as you walk by. 'Beacon Silver' and 'Chequers' have pretty pink to rose flowers.

Essentially a trouble-free plant, lamium will obligingly carpet great areas, even in deep shade. Moist, well-drained soil is best, but the plant will manage even without perfect conditions.

Ligularia × przewalskii

Ligularia

HEIGHT/WIDTH: 4'–6' × 2'–3' (120–180cm × 60–90cm)

FLOWERS: yellow stars

BLOOM TIME: mid- to late summer

ZONES: 4–8

'The Rocket' ligularia

This is an imposing plant for the edge of a wooded area or a shady border that gets some morning sun. No doubt about it, ligularia is a big plant; at maturity, it is likely to be taller than you. The leaves, which can measure up to a foot (30cm) across, are palmlike but highly dissected. The plant is a clump-former, and the erect stems are dark purple. So it has a somewhat tropical look to it. Ligularia needs moist, rich soil to give of its best.

Near the middle of the summer, the impressive flower-stalks appear. They, too, have purple stems, and carry cheery little yellow flowers, each less than an inch (2.5cm)

across, in tall, loose spikes. These last for many weeks, igniting a dim area with welcome color. (Close inspection reveals that the flowers are like tiny daisies—in fact, the plant is closely related to asters.)

'The Rocket' is the most commonly seen edition of this dramatic plant (though it is sometimes listed as a cultivar of *L. stenocephala*). The flower stems are quite dark, nearly black, making a magnificent contrast for the sunny yellow blooms. It generally doesn't grow quite as tall as *L. × przewalskii*, usually topping out at 4 feet (120cm).

Lilium martagon var. alba

White Martagon lily

HEIGHT/WIDTH: 3'–6' × 1'–2' (90–180cm × 30–60cm)

FLOWERS: white bells

BLOOM TIME: summer

ZONES: 3–7

White Martagon lily

It's true, most lilies do best out in the open, perhaps only with some protection from the withering heat of the noonday sun. But here is a modest, graceful species lily that makes a genuinely appropriate and lovely choice for partial shade. Derived from the Turks-cap lily, this white-flowered version has even smaller flowers (about 1½ inches [4cm] across), but with the same highly swept back ("recurved") petals. Yellowish green stamens dangle down, and each petal is flushed with a little soft green at its base. It's an unforgettably beautiful flower.

When this lily is grown well, you can count on it to produce flowers in large quantities, in tiered racemes of as many as forty. One nursery rhapsodizes that "it is simply peerless at dusk, especially when planted in groups of five to ten, creating a grove of candelabras with their glowing flames." Catalog hyperbole? Perhaps not!

The key to success with white Martagon lily is well-drained soil; "wet feet" spells sure death for it (and many other lilies, for that matter). Unlike some, it will tolerate slightly alkaline soil, good news for Western gardeners.

Like its red-flowered parent, this white lily is not, however, sweetly fragrant; in fact, some noses find it unpleasant. But that need never become an issue if you are growing it for show in a semiwild shady area.

Liriope muscari

Lilyturf

HEIGHT/WIDTH: 1'–2' × 1'–2' (30–60cm × 30–60cm)

FLOWERS: purple spikes

BLOOM TIME: late summer–autumn

ZONES: 6–10

'Variegata' lilyturf

If you want to edge a shady walkway or devote a bed to one plant that can be relied upon to always look neat and demand little effort from you, perhaps lilyturf is your best bet. Assuming, of course, that it is hardy where you live — this tufted groundcover prospers best in areas with long, hot, humid summers; it cannot tolerate lengthy, snowy winters.

The spiky, narrow leaves are grasslike but a bit more substantial. White- and yellow-striped versions are available. A naturally compact grower, lilyturf usually remains less than 2 feet (60cm) tall, and some of the cultivars are even shorter (one, 'Christmas Tree', is a mere 8 inches [20cm] tall). Its only drawback is its vulnerability to snails and slugs. So if these pests frequent your garden, be prepared to protect this plant.

As the name suggests, the blooms look like taller versions of those of the spring-flowering bulb *Muscari*, also known as grape hyacinth. They appear on narrow, 10- to 20-inch (25.5 to 51cm) spikes late in the season, and are usually purple, though white varieties exist ('Monroe White').

Lobelia cardinalis

Cardinal flower

HEIGHT/WIDTH: 3'–5' × 1' (90–150cm × 30cm)

FLOWERS: red

BLOOM TIME: mid–late summer

ZONES: 2–9

Cardinal flower

If you have a shady spot with moist or even perpetually wet soil, here's a tall, beautiful native wildflower that will dress it up in style. Cardinal flower is all the more welcome because it blooms later in the season, when most of the color is gone from the shady garden.

A robust plant, yet not rangy or invasive, it has striking flower spires. Perhaps no more than 1½ inches (4cm) long, the individual blossoms have the distinctive fanlike shape you may have observed on the common blue garden lobelias so popular for edgings and window boxes. The species is a fabulous shade of scarlet, but variations can be found if you hunt for them (some are crosses with other, similar lobelias). 'Ruby Slippers' is an especially gorgeous choice, as is the richly hued, more subtle 'Garnet'. There's also a white ('Alba'), a soft pink ('Heather Pink'), a hot pink ('Pink Parade'), and many others.

Flowers are carried on tall stalks that emerge from a low rosette. The leaves are medium to dark green and oblong, are slightly serrated, and ascend the stalk to just short of the blooms. Planting cardinal flower in groups or even broad patches will call still more attention to it.

Lobularia maritima

Sweet alyssum

HEIGHT/WIDTH: 2"–12" × 8"–12" (5–30cm × 20–30cm)

FLOWERS: white, pink, or purple balls

BLOOM TIME: summer

ZONES: all zones (annual)

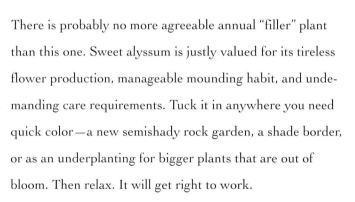

Sweet alyssum

There is probably no more agreeable annual "filler" plant than this one. Sweet alyssum is justly valued for its tireless flower production, manageable mounding habit, and undemanding care requirements. Tuck it in anywhere you need quick color—a new semishady rock garden, a shade border, or as an underplanting for bigger plants that are out of bloom. Then relax. It will get right to work.

If you haven't looked lately, you will be pleasantly surprised to discover that white flowers are just the beginning of your choices. (And if you still want sweet alyssum in white, look for 'Snow Crystals', which has perhaps the neatest blooms.) Nowadays sweet alyssum also comes in purple,

red, and pink, and variations of these shades. Grow them individually or try a blend, which, owing to the flowers' small size and lacy texture, weave a charming, almost tapestrylike display.

No matter which ones you grow, count on your sweet alyssum to reseed prolifically. That is, this year's tidy rows or ribbons will eventually lose their definition and the odd plant will pop up in a walkway, crack, or wall many feet away. In other words, unless you intervene and assiduously yank out volunteers, this plant will play a major role in paving your maturing garden's way to a more casual, informal look.

Lysimachia nummularia

Moneywort, creeping Jenny

HEIGHT/WIDTH: 2"–4" × 1'–2' (5–10cm × 30–60cm)

FLOWERS: small, yellow

BLOOM TIME: late spring

ZONES: 3–8

Moneywort

There are those who decry this plant as an odious pest, never to be invited into a garden. They are alarmists. True, it grows fast and thickly. Of course it will be invasive in certain settings—common sense counsels against planting such a vigorous plant adjacent to a perennial bed or manicured lawn. But if you have a shady area with damp soil that really needs coverage, moneywort will do the trick.

This is a tough plant for tough locations. It even can withstand some foot traffic. So a shady slope or bank with moist soil that has been lying fallow or weed-infested for years might as well be turned over to moneywort.

The plant is actually perfectly attractive. The common name perhaps refers to the rounded, coin-shaped, glossy leaves. The bright yellow flowers, which appear in profusion in late spring and often repeat on and off through the summer months, are between half an inch and an inch (1.5 and 2.5cm) across. Moneywort spreads by means of long trailing stems; it roots at the nodes where they touch earth.

There is a yellow-leaved form, 'Aurea', but it loses its luster in shade (the foliage turns a sickly pale green) and really is better grown in full sun.

Lysimachia punctata

Yellow loosestrife, circle flower

HEIGHT/WIDTH: 2'–3' × 2' (60–90cm × 60cm)

FLOWERS: yellow cups

BLOOM TIME: summer

ZONES: 5–8

Yellow loosestrife

Sure, it can become invasive. But if you simply want to turn over a shady, wild area to just one plant, and you want color practically all summer, yellow loosestrife is a good choice. It grows rampantly in moist soil, but unlike some of its near relatives, it can also tolerate somewhat drier soil, particularly in deeper shade.

The plant's form is a bit unusual. Ever-smaller leaves ascend the erect stems, and the 1-inch (2.5cm), cup-shaped flowers somehow manage to wedge their way in between, also encircling the stem. As they do, they steal the show. Individually, the plants burst with bright color, and a colony of them is a festival of cheer.

Recently, an intriguing yellow loosestrife cultivar has been making its way into the catalogs. Called 'Alexander's', it has creamy white–variegated leaves that help it stand out in the shade and provide striking contrast for the golden flowers when they appear.

Mahonia aquifolium

Oregon grape

HEIGHT/WIDTH: 3'–6' × 3'–6' (90–180cm × 90–180cm)

FLOWERS: yellow

BLOOM TIME: spring

ZONES: 5–8

Oregon grape

In its native Pacific Northwest, this glossy-leaved plant often can be seen growing along highways and in roadside ditches, a testament to its natural toughness. Those settings, of course, expose plants to all sorts of abuse, including poor, dry soil, wind, weather, and pollution. But bring this shrub into your shade garden, and you will be gratified at how beautifully it domesticates and how eager it is to please.

Truly a shrub with four seasons of value, Oregon grape maintains its lush, green, hollylike foliage for months on end. In the spring and summer, it drenches itself in clusters of bright yellow flowers. These are powerfully fragrant and attract lusty bees. By autumn, the plant is draped in small,

blue-black berries, not exactly big or sweet enough to pass as grape substitutes, but certainly safe to eat and attractive to some birds and animals. The autumn foliage is often gorgeous, anywhere from a dusky red to a fiery orange-red, a sensational contrast with the berries. In all but the harshest cold, the foliage will remain over the winter.

Oregon grape would be an easygoing addition to a landscape that is partially shaded by evergreen trees. Its handsome color and texture might also be welcome among broad-leaved evergreen shrubs such as rhododendrons. Be moderate about placement: deep shade may cause it to be too leggy; too much exposure to sun may dry out the leaves.

Matteuccia struthiopteris

Ostrich fern

HEIGHT/WIDTH: 2'–6' × 2'–3' (60–180cm × 60–90cm)

FLOWERS: (not applicable)

BLOOM TIME: (not applicable)

ZONES: 3–8

Ostrich fern

There are good reasons why this vase-shaped fern is popular with shade gardeners. It's easy to grow, it spreads quickly to give your woodland area a naturally lush look, and it is free of pest and disease problems. Its clump-forming fronds are tall, neat, and always bright green. In short, it's foolproof.

Take a closer look at this fern over the course of a growing season. In early spring, you'll welcome the stout fiddleheads. After they unfurl, the outer fronds will reveal themselves as sterile (no spores on the backs of the individual leaves) and rather lacy. They looked like the tail feathers of the ostrich to someone, hence the common name. In mid- to late summer, dark brown, inrolled interior fronds appear. They are a bit smaller and, lower down, are laden with little black to brown spots that, under the right conditions, shed spores on the ground and form new little plants in years to come. Like other ferns, ostrich fern spreads by its creeping roots—new plants may pop up several inches to a foot (30cm) away.

Ostrich fern needs moist soil to prosper. If the soil dries out too much, the leaf edges brown and curl unattractively and the plant struggles. Fertile, humus-rich ground also is desirable. Anything from partial to dark shade will suit it fine. Some gardeners like to plant it with their spring-flowering bulbs and wildflowers because the fronds start to unfurl just as those flowers are passing, hiding and distracting from the end of that show while making one of its own.

Mazus reptans

Mazus

HEIGHT/WIDTH: 2"–5" × 12"–18" (5–13cm × 30–45cm)

FLOWERS: purple or white tubular bells

BLOOM TIME: late spring

ZONES: 4–8

Mazus

This is a very tough, spreading groundcover for partially shaded areas. It can even withstand some foot traffic, so some people tuck it in the gaps between stones on shady garden paths, including flagstone paths where sun lovers like creeping thyme won't thrive. The small, toothed leaves are lime green and grow densely to form a large, impenetrable (to weeds) mat.

Given the reliable, iron-strong constitution of mazus, the exuberant flowering each spring is simply a nice bonus to rejoice in. Hundreds of tiny (half an inch to an inch

[1.5 to 2.5cm]), tubular blooms in soft purple carpet the foliage. They are vaguely reminiscent of tiny foxglove flowers, which is not surprising given that they are in the same family. A white-flowered version, called 'Albus' or var. *albiflorum*, also is available.

The only "catch" here is that mazus must have moist but well-drained soil. In ground that is too damp, there is a risk that the plants will become overenthusiastic. But that may be just what you have in mind.

Meconopsis cambrica

Welsh poppy

HEIGHT/WIDTH: 12"–18" × 8"–10" (30–45cm × 20–30cm)

FLOWERS: yellow

BLOOM TIME: summer

ZONES: 6–8

Welsh poppy

Most poppies prefer to be waving their pretty, crepe-paper blooms out in the bright sun, but this European import is happier in partial shade or in a spot that gets morning sun and afternoon shade. And it is surely a welcome sight there — imagine a glade of deciduous trees, perhaps with some ferns, and small patches of these merry golden flowers spangling the area. If you want even more impact, look for the golden-orange, double-flowered variety, prosaically called var. *aurantiaca* 'Flore Pleno'.

Welsh poppy will grow in soil of average fertility and doesn't mind if it's even a bit alkaline. Shelter from hot sun and drying winds, plus supplemental water in dry spells, of course, is beneficial. If Welsh poppy settles in, you can expect this charmer to self-sow liberally in the coming years, which may be exactly what you wish.

To get started, you can sow fresh seed. However, the contents of packets that have been sitting around for many months or years aren't likely to germinate well, if at all. Alternatively, you can pay a little more and buy seedlings. Once they are up and blooming, you are in for a treat — the flowering continues for many weeks, sometimes all summer long. And, yes, Welsh poppy is perennial, so the flowers will be back the next year.

Mertensia virginica

Virginia bluebells

HEIGHT/WIDTH: $1'-2' \times 1\frac{1}{2}'$ (30–60cm $\times$ 45cm)

FLOWERS: small clusters of blue bells

BLOOM TIME: spring

ZONES: 3–9

Virginia bluebells

Virginia bluebells is a plant whose show is confined primarily to spring, but it is so pretty that many shade gardeners cannot resist it. A native of southeastern woodlands but able to survive much further north, it is easy to grow. The thin, lance-shaped leaves are mainly basal, though a few ascend the stems on short, succulent stalks. At the top of these stalks are clusters of nodding little bells. They begin as pink buds but open to lilac-blue flowers. The blue will be darker in deeper shade.

This wildflower is often touted as an ideal companion for spring-flowering bulbs, with good reason. It likes similar conditions in the garden: organically rich soil in cool shade. Plus, the color seems to go with everything. It is particularly fetching combined with small-flowered yellow or white narcissus.

Like the bulbs, though, its show ends as summer arrives. The stems die down after bloom, and the plant gradually goes dormant and disappears from view until the next year. So mark its spot if you wish to move or divide it in the autumn, and to avoid trampling on it or planting something else over it.

Microbiota decussata

Russian carpet cypress

Russian (Siberian) carpet cypress

HEIGHT/WIDTH: 2'–3' (60–90cm)/spreading habit

FLOWERS: minute cones

BLOOM TIME: summer

ZONES: 3–7

A shrubby evergreen from Siberia must be a tough plant. And so it is. It is extremely cold tolerant, rarely troubled by any diseases or pests, and requires little of the gardener, not even pruning. The color is usually bright green, often turning bronzy purple over the winter. It is not a shade lover per se, but it appreciates some shelter from the glare of midday sun and will do well in settings of light or dappled shade.

To say this plant sprawls may be an understatement. Its goal in life is not to grow up, but outward, and, over the years, you will be amazed at how well it stays with this plan. As such, it has received great praise as an unorthodox groundcover or pathside plant. You might also try it in a shrub border or as a row along the east side of your house.

Although it bears a superficial resemblance to the overused juniper, it is not a substitute. Its cultural requirements are different—not just the preference for less than full sun, but also a need for fertile, well-drained soil. Siberian carpet cypress also has a much softer profile.

Mitchella repens

Partridgeberry

HEIGHT/WIDTH: 2"–3" × 9"–12" (5–7.5cm × 23–30cm)

FLOWERS: tiny, white

BLOOM TIME: spring

ZONES: 4–9

Partridgeberry

This groundcover has an irresistibly elfin look. Its tiny, chubby leaves, sometimes marbled with white, appear in pairs along the trailing stems. The miniature scented flowers are tubular; they are light pink in bud and open to white. But partridgeberry really comes into its own by autumn. Then, the bright crimson berries sprinkle the glossy green mat with festive color. Birds and other wildlife absolutely adore them.

To grow this sturdy little plant well, site it in moist, acidic soil under the dappled shade of trees or deciduous shrubs. It can be slow to establish, but over the years it will spread out luxuriously via runners to form great carpets.

Partridgeberry's rather dainty features suggest that it is best used in a pathside or rock garden setting, rather than relegated to a back corner, so its charms can be appreciated at closer range.

Myosotis sylvatica

Forget-me-not

HEIGHT/WIDTH: 6"–12" × 6" (15–30cm × 15cm)

FLOWERS: tiny, blue

BLOOM TIME: spring–early summer

ZONES: 5–9 (usually grown as a biennial)

'Ultramarine' forget-me-not

As an adorable plant best suited to informal semishady areas, forget-me-not is hard to beat for agreeable character and low maintenance. In spring, it foams with dozens of tiny, blue-petaled, yellow-centered blooms. They have a very appealing, nosegay appearance that is welcome among smaller hostas or any low-growing, green-foliaged ground-covers.

Forget-me-not is not long-lived and, indeed, may not bloom its first season. But once established, it sows its seeds throughout your garden, ensuring that you'll never be without it. To be honest, it can begin to take over, crowding out other plants or moving into open areas. Fortunately, unwanted seedlings are easily dug up and either discarded or moved.

While it is a fairly adaptable plant, it looks its best when growing in somewhat moist soil. It even can take "wet feet," perhaps along the edges of a garden pool or bog. The sentimental legend behind its common name is that a gallant knight drowned while fetching a bouquet for his lady love (crying out "forget me not!" as he slipped under), but you have to wonder just how deep the water was!

Myrrhis odorata

Sweet cicely

HEIGHT/WIDTH: 3'–6' × 2'–5' (90–180cm × 60–150cm)

FLOWERS: white umbels

BLOOM TIME: spring–early summer

ZONES: 3–7

Sweet cicely

Although it becomes rather large and rambling, sweet cicely never overwhelms a shade garden, thanks to the lacy delicacy of its finely divided foliage. Instead, it weaves itself in among other, shorter, plants or makes a pleasant grove along a path, the back of a wall or fence, or in a glade of deciduous trees. Through the the heat of summer and all the way up to the first frost, it remains a fresh, crisp green. Both the leaves and the hollow stems are edible and have a sweet, celery-anise flavor that enhances salads and soups.

The frothy white flower heads, which look like those of many other herbs, appear early, in spring to early summer, attracting the attention of early foraging bees. They're an appealing sight in light or filtered shade, but, alas, don't last long. The small, thin seeds that follow are edible and can be used in baking, whole or powdered.

Sweet cicely prefers moist soil; if the spot you've chosen dries out when summer comes, supplemental watering will be necessary. Note that it forms a thick, gnarled taproot, so plant it where you want it to stay. The plant is best raised from store-bought seedlings or from divisions donated by another gardener, as the seeds germinate slowly and erratically.

Nemophila spp.

Nemophila, baby blue eyes

HEIGHT/WIDTH: 6"–12" × 6"–12" (15–30cm × 15–30cm)

FLOWERS: saucer-shaped, color varies

BLOOM TIME: summer

ZONES: annual (all zones)

Nemophila

Originally known primarily to botanists and native plant enthusiasts of the western United States, this unsung wildflower somehow captured the attention of plant breeders. Perhaps the fact that it is an annual that does well in partial shade recommended it (the genus name *Nemophila* means "grove loving"). Perhaps its eagerness to bloom, especially when brought into the more comfortable surroundings of garden life, had something to do with it as well.

At any rate, you can now grow this low, ground-hugging beauty with flowers in a variety of intriguing colors. Those of *N. maculata* 'Five Spot' most closely resemble the wild version, with white petals tipped with a violet spot and violet veining. Those of *N. menziesii* 'Baby Blue Eyes' are sky blue. But, for sheer novelty, you can't beat two recent introductions, *N. menziesii* 'Pennie Black', which has deep purple blooms edged with creamy white, and its counterpart 'Snowstorm', with black-speckled white petals.

The saucer-shaped flowers are never large, generally only between 1 and 2 inches (2.5 and 5cm), but they are borne individually on swaying stalks, and they cover the plants, nearly hiding the small, scrubby, lyre-shaped green to gray-green leaves. Nemophila prospers in fertile, well-drained soil.

Nicotiana alata

Flowering tobacco

HEIGHT/WIDTH: 3'–5' × 8"–1' (90–150cm × 20–30cm)

FLOWERS: various colors

BLOOM TIME: summer

ZONES: 10–11 (grown as an annual)

'Starship Lemonlime' flowering tobacco

Delicious fragrance is the main reason to grow this easy-going plant. Because they are pollinated by night-flying insects, the long-tubed, five-petaled flowers release their scent at full force when they open late in the day—a plus for gardeners who are away all day at work or school. Yes, flowering tobacco can also be grown in the open, but shade gardeners know this plant's other secret: shelter from the sun's rays coaxes the plants to bloom in the daytime as well.

This justly popular plant comes in a tantalizing array of colors, from red to pink to white to yellow to lime green, colors you will be eager to include in your semishady beds, either individually or in mixed groups. The plain species, freshly appreciated by those who like to cultivate an old-fashioned look in their garden, is soft white with a blush of light green.

Flowering tobacco tolerates heat and cold, and blooms literally from early summer to the first autumn frost. Start the seeds indoors a month or two before you want to plant them outside (note that you should sow them on top of a flat of soilless mix; light hastens germination).

Omphalodes cappadocica

Navelwort

HEIGHT/WIDTH: 10"–12" × 14"–16" (25.5–30cm × 35.5–40.5cm)

FLOWERS: blue

BLOOM TIME: early spring

ZONES: 6–9

'Cherry Ingram' navelwort

Admittedly an undistinguished, mounding plant when not in bloom, navelwort is utterly charming when covered with sprays of tiny, ¼-inch (6mm) flowers each spring. The species flowers are blue with a white center, slightly reminiscent of forget-me-not and pretty enough in their own right. There's a larger-flowered cultivar called 'Cherry Ingram' with flowers that are even deeper blue. But the most desirable version is a true bicolor, also with larger flowers, dubbed 'Starry Eyes'. Each petal is rimmed in palest pink (which fades to white) and has a bold swathe of lilac-blue down the middle.

No matter which version you grow, expect waves of flowers for many weeks each spring. The flowers coupled with the lance-shaped leaves make the plant quite a splendid groundcover for partial shade. Later, when the flowers have passed, the plant devotes its energy to spreading slowly by creeping rhizomes.

As you might guess, navelwort thrives in woodland settings. It prefers moderately fertile soil that is moist. Unfortunately, these are also heavenly conditions for slugs and snails. If these pests lurk in your damp, shady garden, they will damage the leaves.

Pachysandra spp.

Pachysandra

HEIGHT/WIDTH: 10"–12" × 10"–18" (25.5–30cm × 25.5–45.5cm)

FLOWERS: small bottlebrushes, white to lavender

BLOOM TIME: spring

ZONES: 4–9

Pachysandra

Good old Japanese pachysandra (*P. terminalis*): if you have a spot that has average or even dryish soil, in deep, dark shade, few other plants will cover it as dependably, year in and year out. The coarsely toothed leaves, borne in whorls on strong stems, are always a rich shade of green. (The small flowers, usually white bottlebrushes, are insignificant.)

Pachysandra is evergreen in most climates, and may even be seen stubbornly poking a glossy green head out of the first few snows of the season. Try it in your holiday decorations—it holds up well, especially when the cut ends are immersed in water.

If you appreciate this plant but are feeling more adventurous, consider a few alternatives. 'Silver Edge' and 'Variegata' have white-rimmed leaves and are not quite as fast-spreading. 'Green Carpet' has even shinier leaves and grows more compactly than the species. And a related native North American species, known as Allegheny spurge (*P. procumbens*), is gaining in popularity. It is not evergreen, is more particular about soil (it must have moist, fertile ground), and spreads more slowly, but its attractive gray-green leaves are more than twice as large.

Paxistima canbyi

Cliff-green

HEIGHT/WIDTH: 12"–18" × 2'–3' (30–45cm × 60–90cm)

FLOWERS: tiny, white

BLOOM TIME: summer

ZONES: 3–7

Cliff-green

If you're landscaping a woodland floor, you might consider cliff-green an intriguing alternative to the ubiquitous pachysandra. It, too, has glossy green foliage, spreads by means of branching, rooting stems, is impervious to pests and diseases, and requires little or no attention once established. Its tiny leaves are less than an inch (2.5cm) long and have toothed margins—they look a bit like miniature holly leaves. When colder weather arrives, they become an attractive shade of red-tinged bronze.

To look its best, cliff-green ought to be grown in well-drained soil. It tolerates acidic conditions, such as under pine or oak trees. The site should also remain moist over the summer; drought does in this little groundcover.

Because of the small leaves and neat appearance of cliff-green, a flourishing patch looks somehow less overbearing than pachysandra. You might even invite cliff-green into a semishady rock garden. Plant it in a pot sunk into the ground, or remove the unwelcome sprouts from time to time.

Phalaris arundinicea 'Picta'

Ribbongrass

HEIGHT/WIDTH: 2'–3' × 1'–2' (60–90cm × 30–60cm)

FLOWERS: white or pale pink seedheads

BLOOM TIME: summer

ZONES: 4–9

Ribbongrass

No, it's not a bamboo, though if you have never seen ribbongrass before, you would be pardoned for thinking so at first. It's a bushy, mounding, perennial "ornamental grass," valued for its neatly striped blades of cool white and mint green. The seedheads, when they appear, are carried in loose clusters on their own stems.

Able to tolerate even the most wretched soil, wet or dry, ribbongrass is sometimes used as an erosion-control plant on banks or slopes. Partial shade suits it fine and in fact best preserves the quality of the foliage. If it should begin to look raggedy by midsummer, simply cut the plant back by half—or entirely—and await a fresh flush of growth.

It must be admitted that ribbongrass does have a deserved reputation (like bamboo) for vigorous growth; it spreads eagerly by creeping rhizomes. So gardeners who want to curb it must grow it in containers. It's large enough to warrant a half-whiskey barrel or something of comparable size and, when thriving, will be your pride and joy. Otherwise, if massing is your plan, great masses of ribbongrass you shall have.

Phlox divaricata

Wild sweet William

HEIGHT/WIDTH: 1' × 1' (30cm × 30cm)

FLOWERS: blue or white

BLOOM TIME: spring

ZONES: 4–8

Wild sweet William

This little charmer is a world away from its big, bold-flowered cultivated cousin, garden or summer phlox (*P. paniculata*). It enjoys partial or half-day shade and has an informal, easygoing way about it. It is short, topping out at only 1 foot (30cm), and covers itself in loose, airy clusters of sweet little 1-inch (2.5cm) powder-blue blossoms for several weeks each spring.

It also has a wild heart. Its creeping stems take off in all directions, spreading the plant quickly. Some gardeners, therefore, like to use it as a groundcover, on a bank or path-side. It also makes a good companion for later-blooming spring bulbs (particularly other pastels or white ones), weaving the display together while giving it an air of spontaneity.

You may prefer to grow one of the cultivars. Best known is the pure white 'Fuller's White', which has deeply notched petals, lending it a lacier appearance than the species. 'Mrs. Crockett' is lavender, 'Barb's Choice' is baby blue, and 'Louisiana' is rich violet-purple.

Phlox stolonifera

Creeping phlox

HEIGHT/WIDTH: 4"–6" × 12" (10–15cm × 30cm)

FLOWERS: many colors

BLOOM TIME: spring

ZONES: 3–8

'Violet Vere' creeping phlox

Few shade groundcovers are as lovely as this sweet-scented, low-growing creeper. For up to a month every spring, it smothers itself in 1-inch (2.5cm)-wide blooms. The species is soft lavender, but there are many worthy selections available, among them the classic 'Bruce's White', the delicately colored 'Pink Ridge', and the rich gentian blue 'Sherwood Purple'. The fragrance is as arousing as that of lilies, and, naturally, gains power in larger patches.

Because this is such a dependable plant and comes in a range of colors, it makes a wonderful stage for spring-flowering bulbs; the possible combinations are many.

Creeping phlox also makes a pretty skirt at the base of spring-flowering shrubs and trees; it may lap at their bases or trunks.

Creeping phlox's habit is short and spreading. It expands by runners (stolons), but maintains a tidy, dense appearance that discourages weeds from interjecting. You will be glad to learn that, unlike other phloxes, this one is impervious to mildew and is untroubled by nibbling slugs. Fertile, moist soil will encourage it to prosper—sometimes too well. But unwanted seedlings are easily yanked out.

Polemonium reptans

Jacob's-ladder

HEIGHT/WIDTH: 1'–2' × 1'–2' (30–60cm × 30–60cm)

FLOWERS: little bells, usually blue

BLOOM TIME: late spring

ZONES: 4–8

Jacob's-ladder

The small, delicate flowers of this low grower are especially sweet: they are airy little China-blue bells accented with tiny white stamens. They appear in clusters at the tips of the stems in late spring. A patch in full bloom has a fairyland quality. And, since Jacob's-ladder self-sows, you can look forward to an ever-growing carpet.

It is the fernlike leaves that give the plant its common name. They are arranged along the rather brittle stems in pairs, growing smaller as they ascend; they reminded some-one of the Biblical story of Jacob's dream of ascending to heaven on the rungs of a ladder. Unlike with some spring-blooming plants, the leaves of Jacob's-ladder remain all season long.

This particular species has a more creeping habit than the more commonly grown *P. caeruleum*, so it is a better choice for planting in sweeps or naturalizing. Gardeners in areas with cooler summers have better luck with it. In any event, for best results, grow it in rich, moist soil.

Polygonum odoratum

Solomon's seal

HEIGHT/WIDTH: 1'–2' × 1'–2' (30–60cm × 30–60cm)

FLOWERS: tiny pale green to white bells

BLOOM TIME: spring

ZONES: 4–8

'Variegatum' Solomon's seal

No shade garden is complete without this elegant plant— and it will tolerate drier soil. Its strong, graceful stems arch outward, bearing along their length oval-shaped, parallel-veined leaves. Dangling along the underside of the stem in spring is a jaunty row of diminutive, pale green to white, lightly perfumed, bell-shaped flowers. These become blue-black berries by late summer.

The beautiful, sought-after cultivar 'Variegatum' has leaf edges and tips splashed with white markings. If you have the space and want an even bolder show, try Great Solomon's seal (a hybrid of either *P. biflorum* or *P. commutatum*), whose arching stems grow up to 6 feet (1.8m) long.

This plant has been grown around the world for a long time. The source of the name seems lost to history, though there are several theories. If you examine the tuberous roots, you'll see round scars from the previous year's stalks—these are said to resemble Solomon's seal, or signet. (By the way, you'll be able to determine a plant's age by counting these scars.) Another explanation is that, used medicinally, the plant was useful for healing, or sealing, wounds. Yet another possibility is that the six-pointed flowers were taken to resemble the six points of the Star of David, which was once called "Solomon's seal."

Primula japonica

Japanese primrose, candelabra primrose

HEIGHT/WIDTH: 1'–2' × 1' (30–60cm × 30cm)

FLOWERS: color varies

BLOOM TIME: spring

ZONES: 5–8

Japanese primrose

If you've ever seen a semishady glade given over to Japanese primroses, you'll never forget it or cease longing to re-create it at home. Assuming you garden in a cooler climate (they simply cannot take long, hot, humid summers) and have an appropriate setting, you may get your wish. The best spot is one that is naturally damp, though not sodden, with humusy soil. Partial or dappled shade is best, such as under the shade of high trees.

The good news is that Japanese primroses, unlike some of their relatives, are fairly easy to grow. In fact, once their basic needs are met, they will flourish and even self-sow. So you might as well plan to devote a broad area to this enthusiastic plant.

The fabulous flowers line the stalks on all sides, in whorls, and appear in tiers, not just at the top. Individual blossoms are merely half an inch (1.5cm) across, but they are clustered so that there is no missing them. The color range is from white to pink to lavender, accented with contrasting eyes (darker pink or red, sometimes yellow). As with other primroses, the leaves remain basal and are broadly paddle-shaped.

Combine Japanese primroses with other shade lovers if you like, but try to stay with foliage plants like ferns or hostas. You won't want anything to distract from these remarkable, colorful flowers.

Primula ×
polyantha

Polyanthus primrose, English primrose

HEIGHT/WIDTH: 6"–15" × 9"–12" (15–38cm ×

23–30cm)

FLOWERS: color varies

BLOOM TIME: spring

ZONES: 6–8

Polyanthus primrose

These bright-eyed beauties are sure to warm the heart of any winter-weary gardener. Usually yellow-centered, the flowers range from purple to pink to red to white; they are carried in pert umbels of several 1- to 2-inch (2.5 to 5cm) blooms. Enjoy them in pots in early spring, or, if your weather is not too harsh, plant them outside. Tuck some in among the flowering bulbs for extra bursts of color.

Unlike other primroses, these are far from temperamental. They like organically rich soil, and are at their best in partial or light shade. They've certainly stood the test of time—versions of them have been grown since the seventeenth century. Their parentage is complex (apparently a

mixture of *P. eliator, P. veris,* and *P. vulgaris*) and worth mentioning only because they seem to have gathered together the best of their forebears in terms of ease of culture and vibrant color.

Once the flowers pass, you're left with the foliage, which is not especially appealing. The rosettes consist of long, floppy green leaves, almost corrugated in texture. If you're not wild about this phase of the plant's life, or have other plans for the area in which you tucked them, it wouldn't be a crime to pull them out and start over with new ones the next year.

Primula vialii

Orchid primrose

HEIGHT/WIDTH: 1'–2' × 1' (30–60cm × 30cm)

FLOWERS: purple-red spikes

BLOOM TIME: late spring

ZONES: 5–8

Orchid primrose

The poetic garden writer Ann Lovejoy once described orchid primrose in bloom as "a sizzling display of Szechuan fireworks." It's an image you don't soon forget. And this exciting little plant, when planted in drifts in part shade, delivers on Lovejoy's promise.

A native of China, orchid primrose will remind you of neither an orchid nor a primrose. However, botanically it is indeed a primrose, and shares with that group large, paddle-shaped leaves and soft, sweet fragrance. Its form is a bit more like that of another carpeting spring bloomer, grape hyacinth, which also bears spikes composed of tiny, densely packed individual blooms. But these flowers are so remarkable, they'll stop you in your tracks. They begin bright red and flare open from the bottom up, revealing violet-blue interiors.

Moist, humus-rich soil is a must for this plant. To highlight the drama of the blooms, site some of the plants near contrasting-color astilbes—white ones would be nice; red ones will help call out the unfurling show. If orchid primrose is content in your shade garden, it will self-sow.

Pulmonaria saccharata

Pulmonaria, lungwort, Bethlehem sage

Height/Width: 9"–18" × 1'–2' (23–45.5cm ×
30–60cm)

Flowers: blue, pink

Bloom Time: spring

Zones: 3–8

Pulmonaria

Foliage dappled and splashed with silvery spots and blotches really makes this groundcovering classic stand out in the shade. The leaves are mostly at ground level (that is, basal) and lance-shaped, and they grow up to a foot (30cm) long and half as wide. In mild climates, pulmonaria may weather the winter. When planted en masse, it forms an elegant, luminous carpet.

The blossoms, while fleeting, are lovely. They are carried in loose clusters and start out as rosy-pink buds before opening to sweet, violet-blue bells. The most widely available variety, 'Mrs. Moon', has pink flowers that age to blue and more prominently spotted leaves. 'Sissinghurst White' has white flowers. The beautiful 'Dora Bielefeld' has green-and-silver variegated leaves and pink flowers.

Should you wish to combine pulmonaria with other plants, it is an agreeable mixer. It is a good addition to a spring bulb display; the leaves will remain to help disguise the fading bulb foliage. It is also nice with other spring-bloomers, particularly white-flowered bleeding heart.

Sarcococca hookerana var. humilis

(S. humilis)

Dwarf sweet box

HEIGHT/WIDTH: 1'–2' × 2'–3' (30–60cm × 60–90cm)

FLOWERS: small clusters; pinkish-white

BLOOM TIME: spring

ZONES: 6–9

Dwarf sweet box

Yes, it's in the same family as boxwood—and it's no hardier, so is best grown in milder climates. It also has boxwood's signature glossy green foliage, but the leaves of dwarf box are not tiny; they are oblong and up to 3 inches (7.5cm) in length, more closely resembling the foliage of laurels or rhododendrons. And it does very nicely in shade and semishade.

Unlike its cousin, it is a natural as a dense-growing groundcover. It never gets very tall, and while it spreads by creeping runners, it is not aggressive in this capacity. It is never troubled by insect pests or leaf diseases. Probably its best use would be under deciduous trees, where the soil is moist, organically rich, and drains well.

As a pleasant bonus, early each spring dwarf box spangles itself in tiny pinkish white flowers that are richly fragrant—the sweet scent wafts outward and is irresistible as you stroll through the garden. They're not especially pretty, and, indeed, you may have to get close and sift through the foliage just to get a better look. Sometimes, but not always, they become small black fruits—again, you have to seek them out to truly appreciate them.

Senecio × hybridus

(Pericallis × hybrida)

Cineraria

HEIGHT/WIDTH: 1'–3' × 1'–2' (30–90cm × 30–60cm)

FLOWERS: daisies; various colors

BLOOM TIME: spring–summer

ZONES: 8–10 (annuals elsewhere)

Cineraria

A daisy for shade? Sounds unlikely, but it's true. Cineraria can't tolerate full shade, but in partial shade or a place that's sheltered from the rays of midday and afternoon sun, it will grow and flower bountifully. Technically a perennial, it originally hails from the Canary Islands off the west coast of Africa and the Azores. Thus it is not cold-hardy. However, it grows quickly and blooms reliably—so it's most sensible to enjoy it during the spring and summer, pull it out each autumn, and plant new ones the next spring.

Cineraria blankets itself in perky 2-inch (5cm) flowers and is long-blooming. It comes in a wide range of vivacious colors, from royal purple to copper to crimson to baby pink, and some cultivars have contrasting white eyes. You can either buy individuals as plants or sow a packet of mixed colors.

For best results, grow these daisies in well-drained soil, or in pots or window boxes of a light soilless mix. They make nice bedding plants, or can be used to provide spots of color where needed. If kept too damp or too dry, or in a spot that has poor air circulation, they can fall prey to insects such as aphids and whiteflies; tear out affected plants right away so the problem doesn't spread.

Smilacina racemosa

False Solomon's seal

HEIGHT/WIDTH: 1'–3' × 1' (30–90cm × 30cm)

FLOWERS: tiny white stars

BLOOM TIME: spring

ZONES: 3–7

False Solomon's seal

If you're composing a mixed-foliage shade display, don't forget to include false Solomon's seal. It is a relatively tall, erect woodland plant, perhaps better suited to planting among larger plants than some of the other, lower-growing groundcovers. Try it with rhododendrons and azaleas, or big-leaved hostas (it prefers the same moist, acidic soil they do), or skirting the base of a shade tree. Its long, graceful stems are lined with glossy, pleated leaves.

It is known as "false" because it is similar to Solomon's seal (another genus entirely, *Polygonatum*) when out of bloom, though it is often not as large. Also, the flowers are completely different; they're cream-colored, starry, and borne in bowing clusters at the stem tips; later, they become red, not blue, berries. A drift of false Solomon's seal in bloom is an arresting sight—plus, you will detect the flowers' pleasing scent.

Stylophorum diphyllum

Celandine poppy, wood poppy

HEIGHT/WIDTH: 12"–18" × 10"–15" (30–45cm ×

25.5–38cm)

FLOWERS: yellow buttercups

BLOOM TIME: late spring–summer

ZONES: 4–8

Celandine poppy

This pretty, long-flowering poppy grows well in almost any spot, provided it gets the moisture it needs either from the soil or from the hose. Over the years, it will multiply, but it is not as aggressive as lesser celandine (*Ranunculus ficaria*).

The flowers are yellow and glossy, so even though they are small, about 2 inches (5cm) across, they command attention. They make a nice stand under the shelter of deciduous trees, mixing well with other spring-bloomers.

The fuzzy little seedpods (which may be on the plant at the same time as new flowers are opening—a charming sight) are characteristic of poppies. If you leave them be and have no chipmunks in your neighborhood to make off with the seeds, this poppy will self-sow extensively.

The much-lobed foliage seems large for the flowers and is an attractive shade of blue-green that intermixes well with other plants. It looks particularly fine among ferns.

Tiarella cordifolia

Foamflower

HEIGHT/WIDTH: 6"–12" × 6"–12" (15–30cm × 15–30cm)

FLOWERS: spikes of small white stars

BLOOM TIME: spring

ZONES: 3–8

Foamflower

No doubt this irresistible woodland native gets its common name from the way it literally foams with airy white blossoms for many weeks each spring—a sight best enjoyed when it is growing in large groups. You can reproduce this show easily in your own shady garden, provided you have humus-rich soil (naturally found under deciduous trees).

Foamflower's blooms aren't actually pure white. Tiny golden stamens shoot outward amid the white petals, giving individual blooms a starry look and the entire spike a full yet exuberant appearance. The leaves are equally handsome, and carry on well after the flowers are gone, as long as you remember to water the plants during the heat of summer. The leaves are heart-shaped, somewhat furry, and, in the variety *T. cordifolia* var. *collina* (also known as *T. wherryi*), feature accenting red veination. Foamflower leaves gain an attractive bronze hue as cold weather arrives.

This agreeable, good-looking plant is also available in other forms. Among the alternatives you can find are clump-forming 'Dunvegan', with pink-tinted flowers and sage green leaves, and delicate-looking but eager-growing 'Slickrock', with smaller, deeply lobed, forest green leaves and light pink blooms. The vivacious 'Tiger Stripe' features glossy leaves liberally splashed and striped with purple; its flowers are pink.

Tradescantia × andersoniana

Spiderwort

HEIGHT/WIDTH: 1'–2' × 1'–2' (30–60cm × 30–60cm)

FLOWERS: purple, blue, red, or white

BLOOM TIME: summer

ZONES: 5–9

'Snowcap' spiderwort

Because this grassy-leaved, low-growing plant tends to grow in large, full drifts, it is not an especially good mixer. But if a monoculture is what you need in a certain area, it may suit you quite well. It is often used as a low-maintenance underplanting for trees and shrubs.

Spiderwort forms a dense bed of foliage and covers itself in blooms over a long period, often for the better part of the summer. Individual leaves can be as long as a foot (30cm), and they interweave and overlap, effectively excluding weeds. The distinctive, three-petaled flowers, about 1½ inches (4cm) across, look a bit like tricorner colonial hats. In the species, they are purple or blue, but there are many cultivars. 'Valour' is bright red, 'Innocence' and 'Snowcap' are white, 'Rosie' is lilac pink, and so on. All are centered with prominent yellow stamens, which give the blooms an appealing perkiness.

Although spiderwort grows well in sun, it really fares best in partial or light shade. Here, it is less inclined to become raggedy looking, and it seems to stay in bloom even longer. It's not fussy about soil quality, but appreciates some moisture. If need be, cut back flowering stems after their show is over, both to prevent self-sowing and, hopefully, to inspire a second round of color before the season is through.

Tricyrtis hirta

Toad lily

HEIGHT/WIDTH: 2'–3' × 1'–2' (60–90cm × 30–60cm)

FLOWERS: white with purple spots

BLOOM TIME: late summer

ZONES: 4–9

'Miyazaki' toad lily

The unfortunately unappealing common name of this plant doesn't begin to hint as its elegance. The funnel-shaped flowers have flaring or outwardly curving petals that are usually creamy white, speckled and dabbled in violet, curiously evocative of an orchid. These appear in great numbers, all over the plant, singly and in clusters, at the end of the summer and on into early autumn, when the shade garden could use a little color. Because they are not very big, though, perhaps an inch (2.5cm) or so across, they are best admired at close range. So although they can grow further back in a woodland, do yourself a favor and locate some plants close to the path or at the perimeters of a border, so you can admire them more easily.

The foliage, as is typical of members of the lily family, is lance-shaped and has parallel veins. The plant is a clump former, but its creeping rootstock will lead to more plants in the seasons to come.

To get a satisfactory performance out of toad lily, grow it in slightly acidic soil that is evenly moist and well drained. If you're thinking of combining it with other plants, try it with one of the smaller-flowered, autumn-blooming asters — or anything with smaller flowers, so it is not overwhelmed.

Trillium grandiflorum

Large-flowered trillium

HEIGHT/WIDTH: 12"–18" × 8"–12" (30–45cm × 20–30cm)

FLOWERS: white

BLOOM TIME: spring

ZONES: 3–9

Large-flowered trillium

Although this gorgeous white wildflower is a knockout in woodland settings and familiar to many people, it is not an easy garden candidate. For starters, trillium is difficult to propagate. Offsets naturally produced by the rhizomes are few and slow to get established. Tissue culture (raising clones in laboratory test tubes) does generate more little trilliums, it too is slow—about a five-year wait for blooming-size plants. Trillium can also be grown from freshly harvested seed, but blooms may be up to nine years away!

Impatient nurseries and impatient gardeners have turned to wild collection, but this tack is unethical, for the plants are becoming endangered in many areas. It's not the depredations of an occasional admiring hiker that threaten the wild populations (though the plant makes a poor cut flower and is very unlikely to survive transplanting back home). It's the pillaging done by wildflower poachers, who dig up great patches of the rhizomes and sell them to unscrupulous nurseries.

So, needless to say, an inexpensive trillium plant from a local or mail-order nursery should be viewed with great suspicion. Your best bet, if you simply must have trillium in your "back forty," is to check the plant sales of botanical gardens—and pay the high price willingly. Otherwise, if demand for trillium continues unabated, we won't have them in the woods or our gardens.

Vancouveria hexandra

Vancouveria, northern inside-out flower

HEIGHT/WIDTH: 12"–16" × 12"–16" (30–40.5cm × 30–40.5cm)

FLOWERS: long sprays, tiny, white

BLOOM TIME: late spring–early summer

ZONES: 5–9

Vancouveria

As you might guess from the name, this plant hails from the forests of the Pacific Northwest (technically, it honors the explorer Captain George Vancouver). There it can be seen carpeting the ground under redwoods and mixed hardwoods. The good news is that it adapts well to gardens in that region as well as other parts of North America. Though deciduous, it is fairly winter-hardy and grows best in partial shade and humusy, moist soil.

Up close, the plant has dainty features. The tiny, bright green, bluntly lobed leaves are actually carried in leaflets of nine or more. The white flowers, which appear in late spring or early summer, wave above the foliage in airy sprays. Individual flowers are merely half an inch (1.5cm) across. If you crouch down to examine one, you'll see that the petals (technically, sepals) flare back, like the flower of shooting star *(Dodecatheon)*, perhaps—hence the other common name, inside-out flower.

Vancouveria tends to get off to a slow start, but after a few years it grows and spreads vigorously (by creeping rhizomes). An established patch excludes weeds well and becomes self-sufficient, even weathering summer dry spells.

Veronica spp.

Veronica, speedwell

HEIGHT/WIDTH: 1'–2' × 1'–2' (30–60cm × 30–60cm)

FLOWERS: blue or white

BLOOM TIME: summer

ZONES: 5–8

'Crater Lake Blue' veronica

Sometimes the shade gardener longs to grow traditional perennials, not just woodland natives. Some garden favorites, among them certain lilies, campanulas, and bee balms, will oblige, as long as they are situated in light shade or get morning sun. Perhaps one of the best choices is good old veronica.

Veronicas, as you may know, flower in spikes. The leaves, generally lance shaped, are a deep mint green that can get lost in shadows, so planting a cluster of plants works best, as it masses the color for maximum impact.

Among the veronicas that tolerate some shade are the beautiful, gentian blue 'Crater Lake Blue' (a cultivar of *V. latifolia* or *V. austriaca* ssp. *teucrium*, depending on which botanical reference you subscribe to) and the white *V. spicata* 'Icicle'. Both grow quickly in fertile, well-drained soil, but remain less than 2 feet (60cm) tall. The blue one blooms in early summer, the white one a bit later. Both hold their color well when sheltered from hot sun, and flowering may continue for a month or more, especially if you deadhead (remove spent flowers).

Vinca minor

Periwinkle, myrtle

HEIGHT/WIDTH: 4"–8" (10–20cm)/spreading habit

FLOWERS: blue, violet, or white

BLOOM TIME: spring

ZONES: 4–9

Periwinkle

Perhaps you associate this rambling groundcover with long-neglected gardens, cemeteries, woods, and schoolyards, and have never given a thought to its many virtues. It certainly is no trouble to grow, in any sort of shade, even upon the knobby roots of big old trees. It doesn't seem to care whether the soil is acidic or alkaline, dry or wet (though it will expire in downright sodden ground). The foliage tolerates foot traffic and is impervious to diseases. Once several plants merge to form a patch, weeds are virtually banished. All this, and the flowers are pretty, too.

Time to take a fresh, appreciative look at this old standby. The original species, dubbed "periwinkle" because of its soft purple-blue blooms, was widely planted by early settlers to North America. A cultivar, 'Bowles' Variety' (sometimes, and more correctly, called 'La Grave'), is a

more vigorous plant with larger flowers of a darker, true-violet, hue. Not surprisingly, there are also white editions, which bring sparkle to dark corners. Double-flowered ones, which are somewhat fluffy, also are available.

You may be equally interested in growing this extremely reliable plant for its foliage. That of the species is dark green, and perfectly handsome in its own right. The cumbersomely named 'Aureovariegata' has olive green leaves with golden centers (and white flowers), and 'Argenteovariegata' ('Sterling Silver') has rich green leaves rimmed in white (charmingly paired with lilac-blue flowers).

Viola odorata

Sweet violet, English violet

HEIGHT/WIDTH: 3"–8" × 6"–12" (7.5–20cm × 15–30cm)

FLOWERS: color varies

BLOOM TIME: spring

ZONES: 6–9

'Thalia' sweet violet

Some violets are best featured in containers or window boxes, or placed in a perennial flower bed or rock garden. This one is small and grows eagerly, making it more useful as a novel or old-fashioned groundcover. It grows beautifully in partial or dappled shade.

The dainty, fragrant flowers are less than an inch (2.5cm) across, but appear in great numbers, wafting such an evocative scent into the air that you almost forget how small they are. Unlike with some other violets, the flowers rise directly from the center of the plant on short stems. Traditionally light purple, *Viola odorata* also can be found in a range of other colors—'White Czar' is pure white, 'Rosina' is rose pink, 'Royal Robe' is deep, dark blue, and 'Thalia' is yellow and purple. 'Alba Plena' has larger, double white flowers. The accompanying leaves are also adorable. They are heart-shaped and between 2 and 3 inches (5 and 7.5cm) across, well in scale with the flowers.

For best results, grow sweet violet in rich, moist soil and be sure to water if the summer is dry. In a few years, thanks to rooting runners and self-sown seeds, you'll have a sweet little carpet.

Viola × wittrockiana

Pansy

HEIGHT/WIDTH: 6"–9" × 9"–12" (15–23cm × 23–30cm)

FLOWERS: color varies

BLOOM TIME: summer

ZONES: all zones (grown as an annual)

'Melody Purple and White' pansy

For quick and exuberant color in partially shaded locations, tough, long-blooming pansies are unbeatable. They are simple to grow, asking only for average soil and supplemental water when rain is scarce. Purchase bedding plants from your local nursery, or try growing some from seed—the seed catalogs offer a tantalizing variety of harder-to-find colors and bicolors.

Among the many, many worthy types, certain ones stand out from their fellows. The Fama series sports especially large flowers that come in every color of the rainbow. An All-America Selections winner from years back, the charming 'Jolly Joker', has stood the test of time; it has royal purple petals contrasted with a bright orange face marked with purple whiskers. If you prefer solid-color pansies (no bicolors, no "faces"), look for the Clear Crystal series. Or try the lovely, award-winning golden-orange 'Padparadja'.

All of these pansies are technically perennials, but they seem to run out of steam after one season, growing leggy and flowering less. They are inexpensive enough to replace each year, certainly.

Creative use of pansies can bring fresh excitement to a shady garden or border. They look terrific among ferns, are great in rock garden settings or along walls, and provide color when the flowers of neighboring shade bloomers have passed.

Waldsteinia ternata

Barren strawberry

HEIGHT/WIDTH: 4"–6" x 18"–24" (10–15cm x 45–60cm)

FLOWERS: small, yellow

BLOOM TIME: spring–summer

ZONES: 3–8

Barren strawberry

Dry shade? Perhaps this plant is the answer. It's quick to form a lush, low-growing carpet of green, with shiny three-part leaves that look somewhat like tiny, rounded, toothed maple leaves. Good soil is not a requirement; in fact, if the soil is too moist or fertile, the plant can become invasive. It spreads by means of creeping rhizomes and stolons that root as they extend their reach. It is never troubled by pests or disease. Weeds rarely get a foothold where barren strawberry is established.

The small but bright yellow flowers appear for several weeks each spring. They do look like strawberry flowers (the plant is in the same family) but don't produce any berries, hence the name. While the plant is in bloom, it certainly lights up your shade garden.

Although barren strawberry survives cold winters, it does not remain evergreen. So clean up the planting if need be each spring, and expect a fresh round of green foliage.

PLANT HARDINESS ZONES

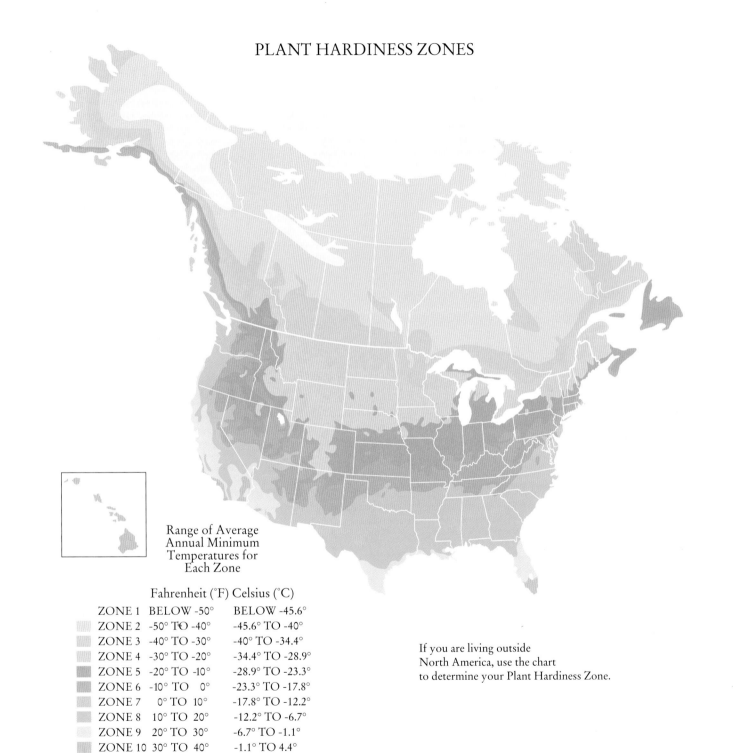

Range of Average
Annual Minimum
Temperatures for
Each Zone

		Fahrenheit (°F)	Celsius (°C)
	ZONE 1	BELOW -50°	BELOW -45.6°
	ZONE 2	-50° TO -40°	-45.6° TO -40°
	ZONE 3	-40° TO -30°	-40° TO -34.4°
	ZONE 4	-30° TO -20°	-34.4° TO -28.9°
	ZONE 5	-20° TO -10°	-28.9° TO -23.3°
	ZONE 6	-10° TO 0°	-23.3° TO -17.8°
	ZONE 7	0° TO 10°	-17.8° TO -12.2°
	ZONE 8	10° TO 20°	-12.2° TO -6.7°
	ZONE 9	20° TO 30°	-6.7° TO -1.1°
	ZONE 10	30° TO 40°	-1.1° TO 4.4°
	ZONE 11	ABOVE 40°	ABOVE 4.4°

If you are living outside
North America, use the chart
to determine your Plant Hardiness Zone.

Sources

Although shade plants are to be found in the offerings of many general nursery catalogs, the following nurseries either specialize in them or have particularly broad selections. Please remember to include the fee for the catalog; it covers the cost of printing and mailing.

Heronswood Nursery
7530 N.E. 288th St.
Kingston, WA 98346
Catalog $5

Plant Delights Nursery
9241 Sauls Rd.
Raleigh, NC 27603
Catalog $3.50

Shady Oaks Nursery
112-10th Ave. S.E.
Waseca, MN 56093-3122
Catalog $4

Underwood Shade Nursery
P.O. Box 1386
North Attleboro, MA 02763
Catalog $2

Andre Viette Farm & Nursery
P.O. Box 1109
Fishersville, VA 22939
Catalog $5

Australian Sources

Country Farm Perennials
RSD Laings Road
Nayook VIC 3821

Cox's Nursery
RMB 216 Oaks Road
Thrilmere NSW 2572

Honeysuckle Cottage Nursery
Lot 35 Bowen Mountain Road
Bowen Mountain via Grosevale
NSW 2753

Swan Bros Pty Ltd
490 Galston Road
Dural NSW 2158

Canadian Sources

Corn Hill Nursery Ltd.
RR 5
Petitcodiac NB EOA 2HO

Ferncliff Gardens
SS 1
Mission, British Columbia
V2V 5V6

McFayden Seed Co. Ltd.
Box 1800
Brandon, Manitoba
R7A 6N4

Stirling Perennials
RR 1
Morpeth, Ontario
N0P 1X0

Further Reading

The Complete Shade Gardener
George Schenk
Houghton Mifflin, 1991

The Natural Shade Garden
Ken Druse
Clarkson Potter, 1992

Gardening in the Shade,
Revised Edition
Harriet K. Morse
Timber Press, 1982

Taylor's Guide to Shade Gardening
Frances Tenenbaum, editor
Houghton Mifflin Co., 1994

Gardening in the Shade
Harold Epstein, editor
Brooklyn Botanic Garden, 1990

The Shadier Garden
Harriet Cramer
Smithmark, 1996

Gardening with Shade
The Editors of Sunset Books
Lane Publishing Co., 1996

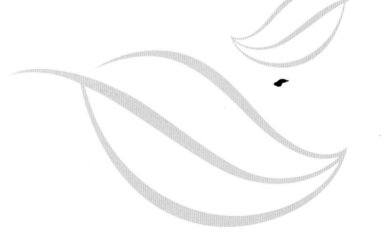